A Unique Management Style for Frontline Supervisors and Mid-Managers

A Unique Management Style for Frontline Supervisors and Mid-Managers

Edward E. Weiss Jr.

Library of Congress Control Number: 2011900760
ISBN: Hardcover   978-1-4568-5399-0
                 Softcover   978-1-4568-5398-3
                 Ebook   978-1-4568-5400-3

This book was printed in the United States of America.

To order additional copies of this book, contact:
Xlibris Corporation
1-888-795-4274
www.Xlibris.com
Orders@Xlibris.com
83037

CONTENTS

If you don't do will soon find out plan you have has failed

Should be done every three months maybe every week on very important issues involving organization

Make small changes, take baby steps that way if change is not working get back to begging quickly

If make big changes is difficult to get back where you need to be. Time consuming and can tie up hands of organization

Evaluating entire process

Putting together what was learned

THIS BOOK IS for frontline supervisors and mid-management personnel who want to learn more about management and leadership techniques, which were developed through twenty-five years of fire department experience and forty-one years of U.S. military service. I was able to develop my own unique management and leadership skills that will be the gist of this book. I was working for the City of Clovis, California, and The Fresno California Air Guard 144th Fire Interception Wing as the base disaster preparedness officer. I was also attending California State University, Fresno full time, which you must carry at least twelve units a semester. I have always thought that a college graduates can make good employees and managers because they started and finished a four-year program. That shows that they have determination and followed directions to meet the needs or requirements of the discipline and made sure all qualifications were met to graduate. University will tell you what classes are required for graduation. It's up to the student to plan his or her path to graduate. That in itself shows management and leadership abilities.

I graduated from CSUF with a 3.8 grade point average. I took psychology and business leadership classes as well as political thought and quotes by *Niccolò* Machiavelli who lived in Italy during late 1400s and early 1500s. He died by the hand of leaders in Italy who thought he was crazy for expressing his views and theories of government leadership and planning for success. He taught not to be a reactionary in life but be prepared to solve problems before they are a threat to organizations. Leadership styles in this book came from heavy influence developed by the authors accessing Niccolò Machiavelli's writings and theories determined to be a solid foundation for developing organizations that are effective and efficient. A *professor* at CSUF told me psychology defines how people are motivated to work in an environment that is set up to ensure all employees feel a part of the organization and are involved in decision making in areas they are involved in.

The book is based on learning and behavior techniques of B. F. Skinner and Maslow's hierarchy of needs in order to establish relationships and lower needs to become efficient and effective at whatever people do in life. *The One Minute Manager* process of three simple rules to be followed will be a part of developing leadership skills early in first-line supervisors and mid-managers. The study of a decision-making model based mostly by the author who developed his own leadership and management skills based on the teachings of Peter Drucker and others is paramount in this book; they believe in delegating the work to be performed by employees and involving them in decisions that involve their positions in the organization.

A well-known general said management was getting others to do what you want done because they want to do it. U.S. Navy and U.S. Air Force taught the basics for leadership and management that can be used the first month of duty to young officers. From then, it is the young officer's responsibility to determine how he or she fits into the squadron or wings mission and develop programs and skills to meet the requirement of the military mission to be successful. This is quite a task, but if he/she uses his/her airman or sergeants from the U.S. Air Force or U.S. Navy sailors and chiefs to learn from and listen to their ideas to get the job done. If an officer is a democratic or autocratic leader, this will be a very hard task to accomplish. If he involves his people in decisions he is involved in and if they feel part of the organization, most sailors and airmen will go above and beyond to complete the mission using best resources be it personnel, equipment, or logistics. Proper prior panning prevents piss-poor performance.

There is a lot to be said concerning that statement used by U.S. Navy to complete operational needs in war and peacetime. If we as people or an organization fail to plan, then we are *planning* to *fail*. The planning in this book is primarily what I want to get across. You can develop a good organization and posses leadership skills budgeting accomplishments. But if you don't develop a plan and continue to evaluate it and change it just a little when necessary to meet end goal, otherwise resources needed for success won't be there, and the organization will be going nowhere fast. This will snowball into personnel getting a lack of confidence in you and ability to perform jobs. They will quickly revert to worrying about themselves and not the big picture required for success of an organization, which essentially is required to be a successful. Most material in this book is based on my leadership and management beliefs.

Listening is very important for you to learn how to gain knowledge. I have found many times I wanted to get up and leave a speech or paper being presented by boring speakers, but I found if you listen for the good things being said, and it may only be one point, you can take it and use it and leave the rest. I managed by experience and knowledge I learned at university. If one of those two things is taken out of the picture, I wouldn't be half the manager I am today. Never have I taken a program and incorporated into my organization as a whole. My leadership and management skills come from pasting and cutting up my ideas and inserting them into a belief and tested management and leadership programs that are above and beyond most. It is based on taking the best of myself and others as well as smart books that make me a good, orientated manager, and I have become that through hard work and determination.

This book will cover planning, organizing leading, and evaluating organizations that will be efficient at what they do. The difference between efficient and effective is this. You may be efficient in anything but are you effective . . . For example, to be effective you have to be efficient at doing the right thing stated in your mission statement, which is an integral part of planning for your organization. It will also cover leadership skills I developed, using the management by objectives for efficient employee evaluations and improvement of job abilities and training. We will also visit tools for good decision-making models, budgeting techniques as I believe the budget is your plan. If you didn't budget to complete your organizations resources to succeed, you have tied your hands, and none of the above programs will be effective until the budget and plan meet together and work hand in hand.

There are also techniques to cut time spent in putting programs together in half the time. There are brainstorming techniques that work better than most presented at this time by other authors in our field of study. There are techniques that will help you deal with stress at home and work. If you are happy at what you are doing, you will do a much better job and will be happy to go to work.

There are techniques on how to train people you supervise to do your job as well as to know the job of the personnel under them. The benefit of doing this is that you are favored by your supervisor for having employees who can do your job so you may be able to attend more seminars and participate in decision making regarding your organization. Everybody wins. We are in a win-win situation, and that feels good.

There are power presentations for getting resources you may need to perform better. It's a short presentation to make the boss or council informed about your program or needs; you will be impressed as others will. This book is set up to be short and to the point. The quicker you or I can get ideas exchanged, you will be encouraged more to learn to be a better manager and leader of men and women.

A few things that are really important have been expressed in the introduction. Let's go onto the meat of the book and hopefully learn from each other. I have found that I learn something new every day of my life and look forward to imparting to you what I have learned so you can make your own decisions, using my book and other authors' books on leadership and management to put a unique style of your own to work.

CHAPTER 1

Planning

BEFORE WE GO into planning, let's look into things I have learned early that other managers couldn't get a handle on. Our worst enemies are going to be time wasters. Yes, there are a lot of them in our organizations and personal lives. They will give us stress that we don't need and cost us time that will take away from meeting the mission of our organization. We need to be aware of who they are and how they may be affecting us as managers and our organization as a whole.

Right up front, I want to say we are not in the positions we are in to ruin time wasters. We want to determine a way to keep them from being time wasters. Let's offer a little caution here. Make sure you don't offend them because you may be ruining a good employee who really isn't aware of what he/she is doing to you and the organization.

You will find that the employee has the answer on how to fix it. He or she just wants to have someone like you to fix it for them. Training people around you helps in two ways: The employees see their importance in an organization and feel better about themselves, and it teaches them to problem-solve issues before they come to you. In future, they will come to you with solutions to any problem be it personnel or production, and just improving overall efficiency of what they are involved in. Now your involvement will be to referee and initiate change by your office. Make sure you set up scheduled meetings regularly no more than fifteen minutes with you and the person recommending changes to ensure what you have done is correct and is getting the results you were looking for.

Make sure that if you do have to change, make small changes. Never make big changes in programs that are new. If you do and find that you are going in the wrong direction, it will make it three times harder to get back to what you and your employees want to be accomplished. Secondly, you have just started training your personnel that what they think is important, and they belong to an organization, and it values their opinions.

Think about Maslow and his hierarchy of needs theory. Once people have met the basic needs like air to breathe, food to eat, and shelter, they can move on to the belonging stage. This is when they feel the need to belong to something, for example, a community or a workplace. Make it your job to know this, and once you bring them into the organization make it work for you. Keep them involved and participating in their work. Find something they are good at and build upon it. Involve them in decisions relating directly to them and keep them informed. This will help you very early on.

Let's talk here about people who have influenced my fire department, military, and business careers: five-star generals MacArthur, Eisenhower, Bradley, four-star General Patton, Lt Gen. Wayne Right, five-star admirals Nimitz and Bull Hulsey. Let's first put this in perspective from my point of view. I will always stop and think about General MacArthur and his wife back in America after a thirty-year absence in the Pacific. He was on the ticket for president, but General Eisenhower became president of the United States of America. On his inaugural day, Mrs. Macarthur asked the general if he thought Eisenhower would make a good president. He replied saying he was the best damn clerk who ever worked for him. I think he will make a fine president. He was not putting Eisenhower down; he was saying that General Eisenhower and later president of the United States was a good delegator and knew how to use people to get the job done.

I can't imagine the hours he spent planning, organizing, leading, and evaluating. His plan was ever changing, and he had to change plans to address them, which meant he never broke the cycle of continually keeping the process moving like I have stated in this chapter time and time again. He knew how to command U.S. forces and all the Allied Forces to achieve victory in Europe through delegating and keeping his generals involved in the circle of planning. That was no easy task to pull off, but he kept doing what he knew how to do best, lead by example, delegate authority, and keep key people involved in decision making that involved them. He was confident in his ability, and he knew how to sell himself and get his points across to others without causing any discord.

President and then General Eisenhower were responsible for organizing the forces under his command to accomplish victory. Many times he found Field Marshal Montgomery and General Patton to be time wasters. I am sure in my own mind that he would have replaced them with other generals who could get the job done. Eventually he did promote Gen. Omar Bradley over General Patton so General Eisenhower didn't have to deal with him.

General Eisenhower saw the fighting ability of Patton; he just had to learn a lesson that probably cost him his fifth star. Patton had a problem with his big mouth. During the Christmas battle of Bastogne, the airborne colonel stated nuts to the Germans when asked to surrender.

It was foggy, and there were no flights to drop ammo or food. General Eisenhower told General Bradley to assemble his staff. This included General Patton and Field Marshal Montgomery. He asked his staff to come up with a plan to save them after others had talked and said it was impossible. General Patton stood up and said he had already developed a plan and his third army had stopped in a battle with the Germans in the south of France and was already on its way up north to relieve the airborne division there. Field Marshal Montgomery immediately said it couldn't be done. Patton had learned a valuable lesson that Montgomery hadn't. He became a team player, and Eisenhower and Bradley were very happy about that.

You see, Patton never had to be told how to get something accomplished; he had to learn how to deal with others and keep them in the loop. He had become a better general and not a time waster. General Eisenhower and Bradley didn't spend a lot of time worrying about him after that. They were off to the more important problem of victory in Europe. General Eisenhower did not have a part in every decision made or control over his generals directly. He was brigadier general at the start of war and was not experienced. He was a great delegator, and it served him and our country as well as his position of commander of all the Allied Forces, Europe, during World War II and later as president of the United States of America. He knew how to take resources available and put them together to achieve the best yield.

He would have been successful at anything he set his mind too. He could have ran any organization after he made the necessary changes and surrounded himself with good leaders so he could spend time worrying about achieving success. I wrote in the introduction that you can be efficient at whatever you are doing. To be effective, you have to make sure you are doing the right things to accomplish your mission and goals.

Developing unique management skills was a must to survive in an ever-changing world. When I was first introduced to Niccolò Machiavelli's theories and writings set in the late 1400s, Italy, I was amazed to see how they fit into modern-day theories. To be honest with you, you have to read it for yourself. Many of today's leaders shape their leadership abilities based on theories and thoughts of Machiavelli.

I am a true Machiavellian and not afraid to claim it to anyone and can defend my position with great ease. In everything I do, I look at my surroundings. If I were in a valley and attacked from high ground, what would I do? Answer those questions by looking four or five steps ahead so you and the organization can deal with it if and when it happens.

I always looked at buildings when I was driving around the town for personal or business reasons, posing the question to myself: "What would I do if I had certain types of fire in the buildings I was looking at?" I would tell fire marshal about things I saw wrong, and he would go out and make changes and advise others. While I was in military, working under Brigadier General Boone, commander of 144th Fighter Interceptor Wing, Fresno ANG Base, I was given a lot of responsibility. He is one of the best generals I have had the privilege of serving under. I would bet everything that he was also a Machiavellian. On the base, I always posed questions to myself on how I would react to various emergencies, natural disasters, and how the base would survive and operate during and after attack and be prepared to recover our aircraft.

I had a very important job. If you couldn't accommodate aircraft, that is to say recover the aircraft, both operations' pilots and aircraft and support for them with logistics and supply went right out the window.

We lose air battle, and we lose the base to fight from. I wrote written instructions that airmen could put in their pockets, and if they didn't know the answer to the problem or wasn't sure, they could read about it in the pocket book I developed.

This left me free to worry about how to solve other problems by always observing my surroundings, determining whom or what might jump up and bite us in the ass. General Boone was in charge of operations, the pilots, aircraft maintenance, and supply operations. I was in charge of the base's ability to survive and operate.

He always said he trusted me as I always made sure he was kept abreast of air base survivability and was in the loop. Good communication skills here made all the difference in making our base one of the most outstanding bases in the Air Guard and U.S. Air Force. You see there is a case of human behavior. He rewarded me for having a good leadership style and gave me more authority. If we failed to survive and operate, the wing failed its operational readiness inspection. During the war, failure of base ability to survive and operate meant losing battle, and that was not an option for our unit. You see the general praised me then; he rewarded me and reinforced my behavior, which made me work twice as hard for him and the personnel on the base.

He included me in all base planning and kept me informed of possible changes in the future that might concern my area of responsibility. This gave me the ability to forecast for the future and be ready to meet any change. You see, I used my personnel the same way he used me as a partner in decision making that affected them and me. He gave me a strong feeling of belonging and that he valued my input to him. The general displayed outstanding management and leadership skills for us to learn a lesson from. I took a lot from him as there wasn't any bad in my area of operation to leave behind. I included Brig. Gen. Allen Boone as one of my mentors in life and a man I wanted to inspire myself to be like.

In 1993 after the First Gulf War, I was *given* the *great* honor of being *the Outstanding Base Disaster Preparedness Officer,* USAF, and entire *Air National Guard.* I received letters of job well done from a four-star general all the way down to Brigadier General Boone who stated I was one of the best field grade officers that he ever had the privilege of serving with. That honor was almost as good as receiving the award itself.

I was competing with some hard chargers, the best of nonflying officers. I had been deployed during desert storm and First Gulf War the year before, and I was able to pick up a few more medals for my contributions while on active duty. Most high-ranking air force officers were quite surprised to find I was a reserve officer. They wanted to keep me after war to help close George Air Force Base at Victorville, California, and move the assets there to a new base and get it set up and running before I left. City of Clovis called me back because of emergency sickness of one of the department heads. I then returned to my life of being a firefighter and military reserve officer. The point here is I had a plan early on in life, and that was not to fail. I wouldn't take no for an answer. I had to prove to myself and others that I could achieve what others felt were impossible. Hope you all feel that way and will be challenged by taking the high road rather than the low road.

When you do this, you will see new things and discover things that will help you in your career and make you a better leader. Life is like a dartboard as I told the people who worked with me. You always shoot for the bull's-eye in life and at work. If you don't reach 100 percent, well you got at least 90 or 80 percent, and I believe that is quite an accomplishment. Quit being a perfectionist and realize not everything is perfect. If you run into a wall while performing a task, stop and come back to it later. You will, maybe, think of things that will make a project better, and usually everything falls together like a puzzle. You need to find yourself a mentor early on, both past and present and start learning what is important in your family, life, and career.

I was definitely Machiavellian in the fire department and military careers, looking behind me left and right, straight forward and above for something that might affect my programs—making corrections to problems with small changes and reacting fast when emergencies presented themselves and believe me they did. I have always kept the planning circle running. I call the planning circle a never-ending process of planning, organizing, leading, and evaluating. They are all important, and to be successful you have to keep this planning circle in motion, or you will fall down and go boom.

Machiavelli believed in keeping friends close but your enemies closer. He believed that you should fight your enemies or potential enemies when they are weak and not when they are strong. It's up to you to learn more about this late 1400s philosopher and how his theories on political taught may help you by giving you more insight in world politics, leadership, and government. All of these affect our planning process and should be addressed. You don't have to identify with him to be a good leader; you just have to follow suggestions reflected in this book.

Read *The Prince* and *The Art of War* and find many articles regarding him on the Internet. I recommend any serious person seeking knowledge of this discipline to take classes at the university level from Public Administration Professors from the Public Administration Department regarding his philosophies.

As you can see, I have shaped my leadership and management styles around people I admire, be it leaders of the past or today. I have become a good listener and have found that the most boring speakers will make a point that you can take to the bank. Point in case, I was at fire department seminar or disaster preparedness convention where they had doctors speaking, and the one talking when I entered could put you to sleep. He stated something in effect that at birth, the human body has the ability to live 150 years. This, among other life experiences, is how I came up with my six ways to live to be hundred years old and have a better life. The six ways are the following:

1. Wake up every morning with the one you love. Get up, look in the mirror, and smile saying someone is going to need me today.
2. Exercise at least thirty minutes every day whether you want to or not.
3. Eat at least one well-balanced meal per day.

EDWARD E. WEISS JR.

4. Wake up with the one you love, with a smile on your face occasionally.
5. Make sure you like what you are doing. Work as long as you can and learn something new every day. We can learn from anybody young or old.
6. Never really retire or go to a rocking chair. Give back to the young some of what you have learned during your life. Do teachings on your profession and give seminars in a local community. Keep giving back, and be a mentor to young people starting in their careers.

Not sure this will work, but I think I am right on target. And live, laugh, and love. The happier you are and the more you laugh have something to do with it I am sure.

When I was working with the Camp Pendleton Fire Department during the summer of 1975, I was working with a retired U.S. Marine Corps Major in the hills north of Fallbrook, California. His teeth were rotten, and I wondered if he really was a retired major. We had a long ride to get to the actual fire we were assigned to, and we were passing through a treacherous country on a road with fire burning on both sides of us.

He told me he was on Bataan Death March, and the road was full of rocks and jungle on both sides. I can confirm this as I was in Philippines during 1970 and saw it for myself. He stated when American soldiers could not carry on, they were beat and told to get up, and if they couldn't they were shot. When in the camp, they received a small portion of rice per day and little water. Some days, there was no rice given to them. Even though he was tired and beat, he always got up and stayed active and encouraged others to do the same, saving many prisoners.

I was honored to know him and proud to call him my friend as he always had something positive to say. Later in life, I thought of him when I wrote wake up every morning, look in the mirror, and say someone out there will need me today.

I wrote the sentence above to a young lady, and she didn't say anything to me like most people I have chosen to do so with. She disappeared, but when she returned, she said she wanted to talk to the man who wrote this. I stated I did and was amazed as to what she said about it after reading it. She asked me what it meant, and I thought she was interviewing me. I answered her questions, and she said this was written by a wise man who was very helpful to others and was waiting for the right person to come in his life. Bingo! That was me she was talking about.

I couldn't believe what she said to me. I was in shock that she was articulate in what she was saying to me. I asked her if she had taken any psychology classes, and she told me know and I recommend she invest some time and do so. As the conversation went on, she acted like she was very sleepy. I asked her if she was okay, and she started vomiting. I helped her and cleaned her up afterward. What she told me shocked me into disbelief.

She said she had been to an emergency room for a very bad illness. To my disbelief, it was cancer. She is or maybe a thirty-eight-year-old woman with two children and a wonderful husband. I have heard that ugly word a lot as I recently discovered two retired fire chiefs whom I know very well; both in their sixties died from it. I said to myself, "why hero Lord?" and held back the tears.

We talked and became friends, and I found she had lost her father a while back. I told her I would come see her when she was going through treatment and be her second father if that was okay, and she was so happy I wanted to cry. I live close by, and I have a doctor friend in La Hoya who I hope will treat her. I will only identify her as Katie the Mary Kay Lady Please hold you're in your prayers as I will.

She was right about me as I was in a relationship and loved this woman so much I would give my life to save hers. Something happened, as I am sure one day I will know. I thought I had been in love before, but I found it in her. I have never felt this way about anything in my life except my grandma who pretty much raised me along with my Grammy, who lived right behind her in Corona, California, the place where I grew up and played among the orange trees there that are long since gone.

Nothing stays the same, does it? They are just memories now. Once you leave, you can never go back again because it changes as I found when I returned from Vietnam on July 4, 1970. I found my brother on a stainless steel operating table with ice packed around him, dying slowly. I was very close to my brother Don with whom I hiked around on the back of my bike because both my parents worked long hours, and when I was twelve, they left the care to me until at eighteen I left home and found another family in the U.S. Navy.

Don was twelve years old when I last saw him okay. I have never shared that with anyone as it hurt me as much at the time as when I last saw the woman I care so much for. When we parted, she said, "You know that saying you say all the time. Don't give up until you've drank from the silver cup."

I said, "You were the silver cup I was talking about." And I have never seen her again.

One of my friends who is a black man said to me, "Ed, love is like a wild bird. Sometimes you have to let it go, and if it never comes back it wasn't yours in the first place." Such a true story as I heard that some time before he said it to me. He is a wise man and knew just what to say to me.

Sorry, I have taken your valuable time up to put that in the book, but I felt I would tell everybody who reads this book just that and get it out of me for all these years so I can heal from that terrible experience. He thought I didn't love him but I did. Thank you all, I feel better now, and I am ready to hit another home run in life and keep giving to others and helping when I can.

My story above relates to me being needed also. My basic needs have been met, and my social and belonging needs are satisfactory, and I am well into the self-actualization phase as stated by Maslow's hierarchy of needs. I still have the need to be in a strong relationship. Case in point, I would be able to free my mind more if I was in a good mutual relationship with a significant other. That would allow me to function at even a higher level of achievement. Can you see how an employee's personal life is important for him or her to reach their full potential?

Last night, I met a master gunner in the United States Marine Corps whom I have not seen for a long time. I walked in, said to him as I pasted, "You look like a person I would pound mud with." And he gave me a funny look as he was with two other people. He walked by me on his way to the head (bathroom), and he looked very familiar. On his way back to the table, I told him this, and he said, "I have been trying to remember where I have seen you also."

As the night went by, I bought him a double of what he was drinking. He left the bar, and I never thought I would see him again. That was the end of that, and later this picture of a true U.S. Marine and master gunner sergeant took his place of honor at the head of the bar where he had a commanding view of all the E-6s and above.

He then motioned the lady bartender as I sat motionless waiting to see what he was going to do as he looked madly at me. He bought a drink for himself, looked at me, and motioned me to join him, and quickly I did what I have done so many times before as that is customary and quite an honor in itself. I took my position to his left as I was an officer and guest in the bar named for E-9s, the highest enlisted rank in the Marine Corps.

He immediately said, "I am buying you a drink."

And I said, "No thanks."

I quickly explained I had stopped drinking four years ago, and he said, "In my bar, you won't take a drink from me."

As we were looking at each other eye to eye, I held to my guns as he insisted and then accepted that I didn't drink anymore. We talked for thirty minutes and had a good time as everyone watched in amazement.

We determined where we knew each other from, and he bestowed another honor on me and said, "You will be at my f—n' retirement if I have to send a jet to get you."

I shared this story right here with you because I want to make a strong statement. You treat others right along the way of your life and keep your honesty and integrity on the straight and narrow, and you too will find people like the master gunner who will want you at their retirement dinners too—duty, honor, country Sempra Fi Marine.

Like he ordered me to be there, and I will be there in full dress uniform as I retire on September 26, 2010, and receive my blue retired card as he will after so many years of service to our great country. I will be his guest and am honored to do so. I am sure we will not lose touch again and be friends for many years to come as his privileged friend and Patrortart.

We did it, master gunner! Who would have ever believed it?

I hope you will become good listeners and planners; if you're not, somebody else will win the prize you're looking for. Look to the meaning that leaders show to you about their need themselves, right up front, but determine if there are any hidden plans that will blindside you and be ready to deal with them. Always ask questions when not sure about something and get clarification before you go forward with any venture. Come up with plans that will meet their needs as well as yours.

Keep communicating in everything; be open and to the point. Don't have any hidden agendas; keep everyone informed of your intentions both up and down ladder and check latterly. By checking latterly with other supervisors and support activities, you will find out if your actions will affect them, and make sure you set plans into operation that will be of help to an organization. Get all your facts, probabilities, possibilities, own situation, and decision or plan of operation when making decisions and planning. Keep evaluating it on a regular basis.

I am a delegator, free thinker, open-minded, caring, and people person type leader with outstanding listening skills. The people I worked with me hand and hand and always top notch. Believe me, they weren't hired that way; they just had potential you or I have to learn that it's our job to teach them good planning skills and how they fit into the organization. You can do this by including them in decision making and planning. You will find many heads looking at it from different perspectives are much better than one. The more your employees participate, the more time you will have to spend, quality time talking to others in your work areas.

Our job is catching people doing good things and communicating to them right away. They will be more secure in their work and will improve their weak areas because they feel good about themselves and know you care about them and where they are working in organization. Happy employees make better employees who will go the extra mile for you when necessary to get the job done. It will make skeptical employees more apt to communicate and participate in decision making.

We have to become teachers of men and women and learn where they are coming from. Are their problems at home that are keeping them from their full potential? It's our job to know how employees are and learn psychology as well as learning behaviors of humans. Pavlov for every action there is a reaction. You have to know animal behavior and understand it before teaching those tricks and obedience.

There always has to be positive reinforcement in learning behavioral techniques. See B. F. Skinner's tips on teaching the young and old. When taking the fifth year teaching program at California State University, Fresno, I had to take a full semester class in early childhood behavior and adult learning based on B. F. Skinner's behavioral theories on how people learn new things and retain information longer. They and I have found that when people don't feel they belong or don't feel confident about themselves, they are not able to grasp concepts when learning and can't retain the information they have been taught.

This tells us something about retaining personnel for our organization and keeping them motivated to do their jobs at or above organization standards. Believe me, if you keep doing positive reinforcement with them, they will perform better and meet the expectations of you and them because you and your employees have identified what needs to done for them to be successful in life and at work.

This will allow them to take more risks by being more confident about themselves and you. They are less subject to being afraid of you, ridiculed, or laughed at when participating in decision making and setting of plans to be considered for incorporation into the organization and work responsibility areas. This will make you and them efficient and effective and increase their potential to learn and retain information. They spend more time on their job and less time with you solving problems they can handle at their level in the organization. They should keep you informed of what they are doing in fixing any problems. They must keep you advised about what they have done and the progress made.

There is much more I could say regarding this, but it will come up in other places in the book. We must now focus our attentions toward planning.

I said in introduction if you're not planning, you are planning to fail. You can see that all great leaders had clear directions of where they were going. We too must chart out a plan and navigate ourselves and employees to find and get to a place we need to be. We will need the schooling and training to achieve our goal and how to prepare ourselves to survive in a dog-eat-dog world. If we intend to survive and accomplish great things in government, military, and business, we have to learn to make the most of the resources we have. The military has to plan at top right down to bottom and back up as well as to keep everyone informed. Everybody must communicate and know their jobs, and if one person goes down, another must know the plan and continue on with it.

Guess what, business and fire departments as well as all government jobs do the same things. The fire department has to be ready to respond to any emergency in the city and render it safe for the public. Their job is protection of life and property. Military has to be ready to deploy anywhere in world. Fire departments must pool their resources to protect state from wildfires and other disasters, and business must be able to adapt its self to a changing world and provide a product that is needed and sells.

Planning requires decisions, and decisions need to be made on information that is proven to be reliable. We need to brainstorm and use other resources to obtain information that can be used for making decisions that will start to develop our organizations' mission statement and goals to get there.

If you already have a mission statement and goals, revisit it yearly, and make sure it is doing what it is supposed to be doing. Don't wear blinders or be caught with your pants down.

I can't say how important it is to keep personnel who work for you involved in any process where change is going to be made. You want them to feel important, so keep them involved. They are your best resource. You need them, and they need you. Don't ever let them think they are being used by you because they will turn on you why because they will feel they were betrayed and lied to. That is probably the biggest and worst mistake you or I can make.

When I was making changes, I used an old firefighter decision-making tool on how to size up a fire and adapted it to military and business too. I looked at my facts first, then probabilities, possibilities, own situation, made a decision, and put it into operation. I added evaluation as I saw on fire and operations and in military operations; it was what made a good plan outstanding. Facts are what you are facing right now, what you can see, but always look for hidden ones that will affect your decision and operations later.

When working with a fire, facts would be the time of the day, weather conditions, heat, and wind direction as well as humidity. All of those will affect your decision on a fire, and you must keep it dynamic and evaluate changing conditions and make change where necessary.

Probabilities are things that may come into play such as changing weather that happens usually but is not a fact. Like Southern California, where you are fighting a wildfire near the coast, and you sometimes have a weather change around 3:00 p.m., and it will blow the fire right back at you. Put that into your plan and make it a contingency.

We now have an idea of what needs to be done. Next, we look at our own situation, what we see that needs to be addressed. Think of structures burning in a downtown area with wind conditions blowing fire into other structures.

This brings up another decision-making tool in the fire department that I have somewhat used for military and can use in business too if you put it into a context that makes sense to you. That is RECEO: rescue, exposures, confinement, extinguishment, and overhaul. We talked about that earlier and will talk about it later too. This is where hopefully we have taken everything into consideration and hold on to your hats because now is where the action starts.

On an emergency fireground operation, I had to see the whole picture and make a quick decision and put it into operation quickly, using the federal FEMA Incident Command System, which really has its roots from military use of battleground organization. For right now, that is enough about that subject, and we will cover it in chapter 2 where we will be focusing on organizations and organizing.

It was difficult for a chief officer to do this in the beginning, but if he or she sets it up right, he/she will have key personnel in important positions later in the fire department and will be free to make sure that the initial decision is taking care of the fire or shall we say the problem.

At this point, he/she must take action and change plans to meet new situations. On a fire rescue, protection of life and property comes first. Then exposures, what's not burned, but what is in path of fire is next. Confinement of fire is keeping fire where it's at and preventing it from spreading.

We can then put our resources to work on keeping fire where it is currently at, and then extinguish that fire and overhaul it and make sure it is completely out. We then revaluate again and put our resources back together to respond to the next emergency.

It was my responsibility to make sure during a fire there were additional units ready to cover another emergency. If I committed all of the cities' resources, I had to ensure there were other resources to cover our city when we were tied up on emergency. This was called instant aid and required prior agreements with other cities, county, or state resources. Here is that term again. Prior proper planning prevents piss-poor performance, and if you don't do it, shame on you because you are planning to fail without plans in place to address every problem in local, county, state, and federal governments. This includes the U.S. military and business; it all has to have plans. You would not believe the contingency planning U.S. military has to do in keeping up with worldwide threats.

I hope you can take the above and adapt it into a decision-making tool for your employees, your organization, and yourself. Use any acronym up you want, but makes sure it covers the basics I have presented here. When making decisions, find facts, probabilities, possibilities, own situation, decision, and plan of operation. Now you need to prioritize. What needs to be done first? RECEO stands for the following:

- Rescue: protection of life
- Exposure: protection of property
- Confinement keeps fire where it is
- Extinguishment: put the fire out
- Overhaul: Make sure fire is out

Now use the above on your problems in business government or fit it into military decision-making process for yourself. Rescue is the most important thing we must accomplish. An example of this is business stopping another company from stealing their product line. That's rescue put into the context of business. Immediately how do we stop a problem from causing additional damage, which is protection of exposures or keeping problem from endangering your entire organization. Confinement is to hold the problem right where it's at until you have better resources to combat problem. Extinguish is putting out fire or removing a problem from an organization. Overhaul means to make sure fire is out. Reevaluate your own situation. What must you do now to get your organization back on track?

From the above, make a decision and put a plan of operation to work for you. Don't forget to include your personnel as they are the most important resource you have.

Everything I do in life I am constantly evaluating myself and programs. I have responsibilities to accomplish. For the good of the city or U.S. military operation and business operating plan, I always am looking at the big picture and how to improve it. Listening skills really come together here. By listening, you can learn how organizations' inner workings influence it as well as outside influences faced every day. When planning, always think four or five steps ahead so you can nip problems in the bud. Think about what you will do when the unexpected presents its ugly head. If you know the lay of the land and what's important to your organization by going through scenarios and probabilities, you will be able to face them head-on when they do occur.

Once you're sure you know the lay of the land, start gathering information for proper decision making. Your job is to serve the organization. If you do what's recommended above and look to organizations' requirements to function at an outstanding level and incorporate them in your plan, you will have a formula for success.

I use the word "evaluation" in this book on a regular basis. It is paramount that we continually evaluate everything we do and make small changes when necessary to meet our goals. Planning, organizing, leading, organizing, and evaluating are continuous and never ending. If you break the circle, everything will suffer, so keep this process working for you, your employees, and your organization as well. I must feel it is important and so should you.

We can easily take what I used to use in emergency situations in the fire department and put it to work in everyday operations. I just put it into the context of a decision-making tool that fits all situations and used it in all my planning and decision making I made for military, business, and local government. That is get the facts, your probabilities, possibilities, own situation, decision, and plan of operation before you do anything. Then continually evaluate it for changing conditions. Tie it all together in your mind, and keep things simple. It doesn't have to be rocket science to make it work. This will be covered in detail later on in this chapter. Did that look like a repeat to you? I thought it is paramount to your organization, and that is why it's represented here again, and I am sure you will see it soon later in book.

Learn how to use and teach people you are responsible for how to use what's known as gilding the lily, which means that 20 percent of your time is spent getting 80 percent of what you are trying to get accomplished. That means you will spend 80 percent of your time making it perfect. I don't want my people spending that much time perfecting something that by the time it's perfected, it may no longer be necessary for an organization to operate with. Think about that 20 percent of your time gets 80 percent of the results.

Stop making things perfect. I told my people that life was like a dartboard. You throw the darts, hoping to hit 100 percent. If you get 90 or 80 percent, is that bad? I say no. I am always aiming for 100 percent, and I will be happy with 80 percent, and then I can move on to the next thing to do on my to-do list.

Caution here: Never fill your to-do list up for a full day's work. Every one of us wants to complete his/her to-do list, but as I have found that something always comes up to consume the rest of the half-day I had planned for.

Before using my own technique, I sometimes felt very stressed to the point of blowing up sometimes simply because I am a perfectionist like a lot of you. Learn how to channel your stress, and I say don't keep the bow stressed because it will eventually break the bow. You too must develop stress prevention in your life. I hope some of things I have presented will help you to work smarter not harder, save time, and be happy in your work. It's important for your work and family to be de-stressed with enjoyment in mind in regards to family closeness when you go home from work. Develop your employees to do the same and be available when they need someone to talk to. If you or your employees do have family problems, it will eventually lower your job performance as well as when they have them the same will happen.

You will be able to spot this a mile away if you brainstorm with your personnel.

I once heard a story about this fish company having problems in keeping the fish moving and more than they could afford to lose was dying to lack of oxygen in bloodstream. No one in the organization knew how to fix the problem. One person who never spoke said, "Let's put a shark in there and see what happens." Everyone laughed, but in the true tradition of brainstorming, they tried it, and it worked. More fish stayed alive, and the shark only ate what it needed.

For brainstorming, break your personnel up into groups and let them pick a recorder. Pose the problems to them, and let them go. Note it is a must for us to look at every solution to a problem is looked at and a statement made back to that group of why or why not the use of their input is being used.

You give them facts, probabilities, own situation, and let them come up with some suggestions before we all can make a decision. Mid-managers should be preparing budgets that will cover their areas of operations. This budget will only get done if you and only you do it, and make sure everything you do fits into the mission statement of the organization. Remember you can be efficient at doing the wrong thing; to be effective, you must be doing what is stated in your mission statement correctly. The budget the mid-manager prepares for his/her operation and monies to improve must go to upper management and he or she must prove its worth to them. Later in the book, I will discuss presentations for budgets and power presentations for use at the middle level.

Let it be said here that when the mid-manager's budget is approved, treat it as the overall budget in your area, and be aware of how it fits into the big picture of the organization. Make sure your objectives here are measurable like the mission statement of an organization, which is the goal of the organization as a whole and is planned, organized, and led to accomplish. Make charts and set times to check movement of objectives, which are subgoal statements made to accomplish your goal as it relates to an organization. If it is not moving along like you would like, reevaluate and make small changes where necessary. It is the upper management's job to prepare the final budget for the organization and present it to shareholders' council's federal government for approval. For state, county, and city governments, the budget spans from July to July. Federal government is from October to October.

Again don't do all of this by yourself. Organize your personnel to participate and let them own some of the process. Involve them in what we have to accomplish. Listen to their highly valued input. When they have contributed to this point, have them sit with you directly and let them make decisions on how to accomplish their work. Remember what we said about happy workers. Set up regular times for evaluations and allow them to own a part of their work environment and have some if not a lot of ability to obtain success or fall just a little short. Never let them fail. This is where we as mid-managers during evaluation meetings with employees initiate change in plan for success.

Doesn't the above sound a little like what young officers are trained to do in officers' school? Remember second lieutenants and ensigns are taught to survive maybe first month on what they learned in officers' school. They have to adapt themselves to own situations and overcome any roadblock and go forward to accomplish their mission. They too will fail if they don't use techniques we have covered in the first chapter. I hope I have hit the ball so hard that you will never forget how important planning is—plan, organize, lead, and evaluate. Tie those four words together and never stop doing any one of them. Don't think it's over when you have done this once. It will never be done, and the importance you give it will determine your success and the organization's.

Let's reemphasize involving your personnel at all levels, and let them participate in decisions influencing themselves and parts of the organization they are responsible for. Set meetings with them to discuss any problems or delay of programs. Nip problems in the bud, and come up with changes to meet any roadblocks to your and their programs' schedule to be completed on time.

Keep looking and listening to see where you can best serve the organization now and in future. Make yourself and employees so valuable that the organization cannot function without you or them. Don't hide any secrets and be open to others. I believe employees below me should know my job and the persons below them. I should know the job of the person below me as well as all jobs in area I am responsible for. Be seen and keep in touch with your people. Ask upper management if you can start to learn necessary job requirements for you to succeed in the first few months in that position.

After you are in upper management for three months, you better start showing results, some results, but you need to listen to what's going on in the new job, and make it your business to know and keep abreast of areas you are responsible for. Be careful and don't change anything until you are well informed. Then you just make small changes, watch where it gets you. Reevaluate, and when you find something that works, start going forward, keeping people informed and involved. Don't worry; it's not that hard if you use the simple management techniques I have shared with you in the first chapter.

If the manager above you is sharp, you should be performing work that wouldn't be available to you in other positions. I did this to train personnel below me, and it always paid off in the long run. It's all up to you. Are you ready for the challenge? You have heard how I have developed my unique management style, and believe me you will learn more in the chapters that follow. This is just the beginning of a long career in whatever field you are in. Look around you, listen to what's being communicated up and down the chain of command as well as the latter, and evaluate and see where you fit in, and don't burn any bridges.

To close, I think about this maybe ten times a day. Drive it home, U.S. Navy. Prior proper planning prevents piss-poor performance. That says it all, and I want to thank the U.S. Navy for the best memories a man could ever have. I am not leaving the USAF out. There are some fantastic personnel in that organization that changed my life. I want to thank most of all, again, Brigadier General Boone and Brig. Gen. Eddie Aguirre, past commanding officer 144th Fighter Interceptor Wing, Fresno ANG for having faith in me and offering me the chance to go to officers school.

Let's start to organize the decisions and the planning we have done in this chapter in chapter two.

CHAPTER 2

Organizing

ORGANIZING IS FAIRLY simple once you have determined what you want to accomplish. You did that in the planning phase. The time we spent making sure we had a good plan can now be fitted into the organization for maximum results. When I visited air force bases during inspections and for reviewing my base's plan, I found that each base, depending on its higher authority, was given the end result and guidelines to follow. The U.S. Air Force allowed each individual base to come up with varying programs. Remember they had to have the basic program to be recognized. Those varying programs organized at the base level determined whether the bases' programs were excellent or outstanding. All the bases I have served at where I was responsible for organizing base plans to survive and operate were outstanding, the best rating the U.S. Air Force gives for operational inspections. I didn't do all that myself. I trained personnel around me to think for them and not to be afraid to tell me what they thought. STAT rating is given to bases meeting the minimum standard.

Start putting all of the information around you into some magical light bulb, and the light should be coming on right about now. Don't worry if it hasn't because it will. Military allows for free thinkers in its lower commands; the fire chief gets responsibility to organize and business to organize, to get whatever they are selling in the hands of the consumer.

Organizing is then putting your organization in such a state as to maximize its resources, man power, equipment, and logistics to meet the mission statement of an organization. For example, it will be the job of first-line supervisors and mid-managers to take directions from above and streamline their operations so they improve overall performance of the organization.

At this point, I want to talk about the information going up and down from the organization and how it is so very important to have lateral communication as well. We talked in planning on how very important it is to have communication down from higher authority and up from the lowest level of operation. I want to emphasize here how important everyone in organization is to overall operations during emergencies and nonemergencies. The guys changing light bulbs and emptying trash give us the ability to spend our time best by forecasting needed changes in future and being ready for it.

Train our personnel to be free thinkers and operate in an environment that they can achieve in and improve overall operations of their area. It is also important that these personnel communicate latterly to counterparts with what you're doing that may affect them and vice versa. Help each other and keep things simple. Make changes where necessary and evaluate results. Make sure your change is measurable and can be tracked for the highest yield. Put that change into operation and start organizing for maximum results.

I hope you start realizing again how important planning is to me and you if you want to be more than successful. Be happy in what you do. If you don't want to move up ladder, it is all right to stay where you are at. Caution: Don't grow stale there.

Challenge yourself and employees to find or always be looking for better ways of doing things. Incorporate into your plans and also train employees below you so they have necessary tools and requirements to promote. By this time, you should be realizing we are starting to delegate, teach our personnel responsibilities, plan organizations around our resources, men and materials necessary, to complete our overall operation to meet the needs of business and citizens to survive in the world of today. In a nutshell, our job is we provide business to local government or federal and department of defense with resources for action.

Along with my own experiences, I came up with my own management style by mixing and matching from best of everything I saw out there. Prof. Tom Bream, a psychology professor at California State University, Fresno, saw that I was taking seventeen units in upper division classes at California State University, Fresno, all psychology and public administration plus working fulltime for City of Clovis and California Air National Guard, Fresno, with family of seven.

These were classes that would break or make my 3.8 plus grade average. First, he told me he couldn't achieve what I was doing. I thought it odd he came to me. Could this man care about me? To begin with, he was using psychology to show me someone really cared about me.

That motivated me to talk to him about all the concepts of psychology. He once said to me, "Where does leadership come from?"

"Well," I said, "from concepts I learn from reading books and am taught."

He said, "Are those concepts facts?"

He told me facts are easily disproved, and before it was a fact, it was a theory. To be theory, it had to be proven by three separate studies producing the exact same results under lab conditions. He asked how I knew what I was looking at and perceiving was what he was seeing. We as people can have a theory about what we see, but we cannot prove it scientifically as which would make it a fact. Reason for that is that there is nothing for us to measure; it's all perceived. Professor Bream continued to challenge me during my stay to learn more about psychology. I came away with respect for psychology and what I could learn from it and put in my bag of tools to keep. Now I want to share all of that as we organize ourselves while still doing the circle of planning.

Professor Bream sparked my interest to learn more about psychology and behavioral study of man's needs to learn, provide shelter, and have a sense of belonging. We all have essential needs within us; people can have individual needs, but they must meet the basic needs first according to Maslow's theory of needs.

I am not a follower. I go my way, and if you don't like that, don't waste my time trying to change me. My beliefs come from instincts, and some learned ability that really makes sense to me. My son Edward, the fourth, actually called me the other day and said some person said he couldn't do something. I waited for the time he was really listening and said, "Eddie, no one can tell me I can't do something as long as it isn't against law. You tell me I can't, and I will find a way to do it."

He stated, "That makes sense, Dad."

I also told him to go back to this person with solutions he can use that only my son could provide. I hope my son learned a lesson to listen like I want all of you to do. Listen, come up with a plan, organize, lead, and evaluate.

This is something anyone in the organization can use. Be your own thinker, but listen to others around you, above you and below laterally and outside your organization. Keep abreast of world affairs and how they relate to you. Look to see what might be out there as well as what could affect your organization.

Teach others around you to be free thinkers who can excel to whatever position they may want. Be happy if they are promoted above you because you developed them, and that says it all. Keep your friends close and your enemies closer. Watch them if you know who they are. Keep focused on the goal you planned and are starting to organize for now.

Find out what makes you tick and how best to develop yourself to maximize for best performance of your true abilities. Remember, as a man or a woman you can perform at least twice as much as you believe possible. Go to a university again if you have to. Take public administration classes if you dare to because you really won't learn this in most business related classes.

I know I took business classes and was taught concepts not roots of leadership that I could develop myself for killer results. I found who I really was at CSU Fresno and want to thank Prof. Tom Bream who saw potential in me and went above and beyond to make sure I knew my psychology theories. I want to thank Professors Chaw and Franks who taught me budgeting, theories of Machiavelli, organizing, cutting, and pasting programs together for maximum results, to name a few. It was really hard but worth it in the end.

Organization models will show us that they can start very small and expand quickly to handle the needs of an organization and people we serve. In business, the goal is to provide a product that a consumer can use at the least possible cost. In government, be it federal, state, or local we are in the job of protecting life and property and providing public services at the lowest price possible but keeping our services efficient and effective.

I found in military and city service as well as state in California Air National Guard and being designated military on scene commander for Central California in regards to disasters that organizing is important after you have good plans to work with.

We needed organizational structures that were capable of expanding quickly. I personally found as a young firefighter in Southern California that the public safety especially fire department was behind the times as far as having communication links and good organizational models that could be expanded quickly or shrunk as the disaster calls for it.

This was not just me; it was confirmed by a local fire chief in Southern California, my own father. I also developed the first disaster plan for City of Clovis, California, and was in charge of preparing the city for response before, during, and after the disaster. That took a lot of organizing as we changed our chain of command in different departments to accommodate our plan.

I have had a lot of experience in this area, and I now challenge you to take a magic carpet ride with me and learn some of my techniques and concepts for organizing for maximum results.

People, I must keep this simple, so I will quickly show you how fast your organization can expand to the needs of the people it serves. In federal arena as well as state and local governments, we use what we call the National Incident Command System in the beginning and now it is called Federal Emergency Management Agency Command System (ICS) used by federal government and states. So from state to state, city to city everyone is using the command system for fires, disasters, and unrest.

Military already has a command system. FEMA's system initially was adapted from military use. Organizing for maximum results allows others to use ideas learned from past fires, disasters, and unrest. The fight on terrorism being conducted by our great nation now is under the department of homeland security, and FEMA falls within that organization.

Now you can see why it is important for federal, states, local government, and U.S. military to fall under this command structure and hit the ground running. Like they say, I love it when a good plan comes together. You know and I know that things come together for a reason. You would not believe the amount of time spent by U.S. military on contingency planning.

They have a constantly changing world with threats popping up like popcorn. The FEMA command system is designed to have one person responsible for five others. The CEO in a business can supervise five to seven department heads. This depends on those he or she is supervising and can be more in a business, contingent on the people and experience they have in an organization.

Those department heads supervise another five to seven and so on as the organization gets bigger at bottom and smaller at top. When any manager trains his or her personnel to participate and own what they are doing, you will find they can supervise more people. This is true at any level in any organization and is very true at the frontline supervisors and mid-manager's level of the operation.

The better you develop your employees with suggestions made to you in this book, the easier your job becomes, and you can supervise more people and still get your work done because you and your personnel become a team that will operate efficiently and effectively on the work that needs to be accomplished to provide an outstanding yield for your organization. This is true in business, military operations, and governments. You will find the higher-up in any organization, the general/admiral, CEO, city manager, and so on can supervise more people and be effective at what they are doing because they have highly motivated people who have been well trained on where the organization is going and what they have to accomplish to ensure they will get there. They are pretty much doing the planning and managing people in their own department or division. They can also supervise more people at the upper management position of branches, sections, or subdivisions or whatever your organization calls on them to do.

This will depend on how large your organization is and the support it needs to operate at an optimal level. These could be a sales branch, logistics, planning, personnel, finance, maintenance, and so forth. Sales branch or supply branch will not usually be in your chain of command. They operate separately to serve the needs of the organization, and most of the time they report directly to a department head. They are important to frontline and mid-managers because things they do and things you do can upset the applecart and cause confusion. Maybe this is the information they need to track personnel or planning and forecasting. Or information frontline supervisors and mid-managers need to ensure they have resources they need to keep their part of organization efficiently and effectively.

Once the organization gets down to the mid-manager level, he may be supervising five to seven frontline supervisors, and if he or she has done his/her job right more depending on requirements of jobs being done. There is more factory work and less precision work if the frontline supervisor is needed to work on line or inspect parts or any goods being made. In military or government, a frontline supervisor maybe able to supervise five to twelve personnel. All of this depends on how those personnel are trained, as I hope, to participate in decision making at their level that affects their jobs and work area, find things they like to do and put them to work doing it.

One of the employees might like to work on computers. The mid-manager can sometimes pull him/her in to put together programs that will help the supervisor to get information he or she needs. That will make the frontline supervisor happy because he or she gets the needed information that is needed to do the job easier. The employees are happy because they get to spend some time working on computers and feel better about themselves because they are contributing a valuable service to the organization and are recognized for it. Remember the general did that to me, and I worked twice as hard for him and would not accept failure as an opinion. Who knows they may be promoted to computer programmers in the organization. This will be a situation where everybody wins right on up to the mid-manager's level because he/she gets information quicker and maybe he/she will have more use for the employee working on computers.

His/her behavior has been seen and he/she has been praised for it and the behavior has been reinforced by more responsibility and hopefully a pay raise.

Now all of you should be getting an idea of what training your personnel, to participate and be involved in some decision making, can do for you and the organization. When a pay raise can't be given right away, studies in behavioral science have shown just caring about an employee will motivate them to do more.

The frontline supervisor will gain favor of the mid-manager, and it will go right up the ladder to the point that there is a full-time position for the employee working on computers for a mid-manager and other frontline supervisors possibly. The section/division manager will see this, and all will be praised for developing and motivating personnel who are above and beyond the norm.

The employee will eventually receive a raise as he/she makes himself/herself more valuable at that level. Now your mid-manager's position and those below you become so valuable that the organization can't operate without your services and will ask other mid-managers to come see your programs and design theirs after what you have done, and that is the recognition you want.

Other employees will see the results of what happened to their fellow employee and will work to improve themselves. This will happen to employees who resisted joining in when first asked to participate. Now as before, your job is to find people doing well and tell them as soon as possible what you observed them doing and praise them for doing it. We are now to point that are part of organization has happy employees and supervisors and that makes all jobs easier including frontline supervisor and mid-manager's job too.

You are doing things that will help you and your employees get promoted to frontline supervisors in other parts of organization and so forth right up the ladder. Don't worry about training other people to do the jobs of supervisors you have lost as it reflects upon you and your ability to manage and lead. You will have to spend some time with them to get them orientated to your style of management. Then they will fit in and start doing above average jobs as they see others around them doing it.

No one wants to be the worst, but you will have them. Be aware of this as you will have to treat them different. As I have mentioned before, everyone is different; you just have to learn what makes them tick and use that information to manage them to succeed.

If you maintain the level of your planning, organizing, leading, and evaluating, make it endless, for example, the planning circle. At this level of performance, who knows the sky's the limit and your promotions depend on how determined you are to work hard and long hours you put in.

The supervisor must have an agreement made with employees as to job requirements and meet with them quarterly to review their work and a final evaluation at end of the year. The supervisor should use the management by objectives evaluation, which requires the employees to fill out their own evaluation and then meet with the supervisor to discuss results and determine what overall evaluation will be.

I will ask the question that just popped in my head, "Where do you want to be in that organization?" I want to be at the top with other movers and shakers. Knowledge is power, and power to me says I can't have it unless I surround myself with movers and shakers.

I want to see all of you at top, but the world and life doesn't work that way. There just isn't enough room at top for all of us. Don't be discouraged about that. Life is like a dartboard; if you don't shoot for the bull's eye, you want get the 80 or 90 percent mark and that is fine by me.

Find your notch in the organization because everybody is good at something and the job at the top will be to find those people and get them where they will be happy. Everything we have just discussed is true in federal, state, city, and department of defense. I am comfortable in any of those organizations. Give me a job to do, and I can perform it. You need to determine where you now fit in, and if you want to go up, be more dynamic. I am slowly showing you a way. It is true in business too as they do the same thing.

Back to our organizational tree or FEMA's Incident Command System and the organizational tree for business and governments when opening during nonemergency conditions. It is designed to inflate and deflate do to supply and demand. It is in place to protect and serve the organization you are employed in.

We can now see why our organization can be small and grows slowly but should be designed to grow quickly if necessary or deflate when the economy dictates so or during disaster when things finally quieten down. Now let's look at where you are at in an organization and what you should be doing to fine-tune yourself and others to best serve the organization.

Well, we planned our hearts out, and we are sure our plan won't fail. There are evaluations in place to insure it won't. We have learned enough about our organization and know where we fit in it. We have designed plans for our part of the organization. Further, we have started to train those around us to participate in decision making. Learned people have needs as well as we do. Started to learn a little about leadership and behavioral science to know how to treat people and get them rowing with us not against us. They are even coming to you with solutions to fix problems and are willing to carry them through to completion.

Suddenly you are starting to have a lot more time lately. Is it because it's the time of year? I think not, I would believe the organization is running more smoothly because we planned, included people, and showed we cared about them not through talk but action.

Now we set back and do nothing more. I think not I want to be on top; how about you? I am going to see where I can do more for my organization with the employees I have developed and especially the ones who are eager to go higher.

Behavioral science shows us that people have needs as we do. Help them find out what they need to reach their full potential and give them a chance. So far, we have organized ourselves pretty good, and as good managers should, we are going to schedule time to just look at our part of the organization and the whole to see if we are still doing what needs to be done.

I didn't say evaluate, but I think you got the idea. Then change our direction using small changes. Now we are off, looking for a better way to invent a light bulb or cure world hunger. You know what I mean; look around, find direction, and put your nose to ground. Let's produce and make sure we are noticed for the good things we are doing.

They may not say anything, but as long as we know what we did, we are happy. Let's not forget our people, recognize them for their contributions, make sure it goes in their evaluations. Organize for results you and only you know what information you need to make decisions that will make your part of the organization strong.

You need to be like thunder and lightning when you do this. Don't get too chesty, but you are going to be your own best advocate. Remember there are still people out there who will and can stab you in the back. Be aware of that and your surroundings, but don't let it slow you down. Keep going as they will get there come upping as people see what they are really all about.

I hope you are doing this now, but let's talk about it here. We need to prioritize our inboxes where information comes from above, below, and laterally. All of this is information you need from an organization to function in it. You will also get info from outside the organization if you are smart. This may include but is not limited to professional journals, Internet articles, and info from friends and associates relating to what they are doing. This is where networking is an excellent source of information. Remember, take the good and leave the bad. Take and give cards out at professional seminars or speeches. Join local organizations. The professional people don't have to be in your particular profession. You will get lots of information there. Learn to be a salesman. Salesmen always have to keep closing and getting new deals in their pipeline to keep getting paid. We are all salesmen who are selling ourselves every day to other people and our bosses. This is true for university professors, lawyers, doctors, business men, and the blue-collar worker on the street.

Have an inbox on one or the other side of your desk. Put three other boxes on other side labeled priority, important, good information. Work on priority box. When you're done with that, go to important box. If you don't use important and good information boxes, empty them at least once a week. You can screw things up here, so anything that comes from top for your review is priority. Also information that comes to you latterly, for example other departments that have information you need to function, should be read and answered. Also information from below will be a priority to you. Information from outside organization can wait, and you can file it for future use. Don't forget it; some ideas may make more sense to you later. Schedule time in future and put it on calendar. Guess what you do with other incoming mail.

Also prioritize your e-mail the same way. If you don't open any e-mail for a long time that is in your nonpriority box or whatever you want to call it, open it, and if it is not important, delete it. Don't leave a lot of e-mail in your inbox for a long time. It will become a time waster for you as you will not know the information in them, and you will eventually have to open every one of them. Read informational messages right away. Make a note on them, and put on computer calendar with bells and whistles to alert you before and when report or meeting is due. This is also true if you have to write a report to someone in the organization within a certain amount of time.

I hate long e-mails that tell you more than you need to know. Be precise and to the point. Answer five Ws: who, what, where, when, why, and how. If you have to write more than two paragraphs, it should probably be a well-prepared report.

The computer is a time-saver for you if it is used right, garbage in garbage out. Don't be the one who wastes other people's time. Maybe if you start doing that, it will catch on. Top managers don't need to have their time wasted as they don't have time available to do such things.

Your writing skills and being to the point will bring you praise. Also don't waste people's time on phone; know what you need to ask before you call. Get that information, and clarify you understood what was said by briefly repeating it. When the boss says yes, get off phone quickly. You can say, "Boss, I am really busy. And that is all unless you have other questions you want me to answer." That puts everything back in the boss's lap. If he/she wants to talk, he/she just might be showing you he/she cares about you, and your work is being recognized in the organization.

Start getting organized with your written reports and e-mails as well as communication skills. When you do have to communicate orally, know what you are going to say and practice it a lot before the presentation. Tell them what you are going to tell them; tell them, and retell them. And ask if they have any questions. Know the answer to questions they may ask, and be prepared to answer them. This is all the time you will get. Make your presentation five minutes exactly with ten-second lead time before or after. If you can't do that, maybe the presentation isn't important.

Organize personnel for working on special projects. You know your organization and what will work. I used to put personnel in a group and had them select someone to record and report information. Also a chairman to make sure the group stays focused. I would talk to the group about what I was thinking about, but I always left it open for them to come up with their own ideas.

They then reported to me, and together we would decide how best to put the new program to work. From there, we assigned job responsibilities and scheduled time for the project to be accomplished. Keep it simple, stupid, and don't do all the work.

You see how you are becoming a leader and voilà your personnel are happy and you are too, and they will never lead you down the wrong path. Someone great once said, "Management is getting people to do what you want done because they want to do it." People say that came from President Eisenhower, and I think it did.

Make your to-do list efficiently and effectively. Remember, you can be efficient at doing the wrong thing. We need to be effective at doing the right thing. Make sure you have a to-do list for each day that meshes with what you need to accomplish during weeks, months, and years.

Be sure to schedule monthly and yearly to-do lists with bells and whistles on your calendars. Make sure you take time to evaluate the to-do lists. Yes, there is that terrible word again. Make sure you don't have to change things a little to meet your needs and the organization's. Also only schedule half your time. Don't make a mistake and schedule all your time.

Remember, I said the other half will be filled with other projects you are not aware of. Be quick on your feet. Be prepared for the worst, and you will never go wrong. Let's get ourselves organized, and we do that by setting up our organization's organizational tree to show the chain of command and responsibilities assigned to CEO, department heads, branches, sections/divisions, subdivisions, right on down to workers at entry level. The military and government have the same thing with different names for all levels.

I am going to put report writing here. It is easy to write a report if you follow some of my basic rules. First, determine what your subject matter is. Subject can be memo, informational, and briefing. A report should be short and to the point. A wordy report can do nothing but add more questions and cause confusion to the reader.

First, answer these questions: who, what, why, when, where, and how. Those are called the five Ws and must be answered in a memo. For a briefing, answer five Ws and also tell them what you're going to tell them, tell them, and retell them in that order. You must get your point across quickly. This should take no more than five minutes to read.

You can also use this format to brief people above you and below you too. This is usually used to gain something you need or to make a proposal to improve operational performance. Take only five minutes and practice it to point; it takes no less than ten seconds below or above five minutes. Remember this is an informative briefing, and you have to get your point across and win support for it. If you blow this opportunity, it may be gone forever.

Be ready and tell them what you're going to tell them. Tell them, and retell them. I know I covered that in this chapter, but it is very important to do this right. This will get you what you need to do your job, or you might get less because you didn't cover key aspects to win their approval on what you needed.

If you don't get what you need, go back, reevaluate, and work with what you get. I was always thinking about how to get things I wanted through creative thinking. Our training crew wanted to buy video and audio equipment that would allow them to put out professional quality CDs and tapes. We didn't have the money in my budget, and I knew the fire department couldn't justify the expenditure to get it.

I thought about it for about a week and came up with a plan to present it as an expense to our disaster preparedness budget. We justified it by saying we could use it to give interviews about what the city was doing during a disaster drill. So the city manager could use it to brief the press on what the city was doing to combat a scripted disaster drill when it called on her to update city council and citizens of Clovis though the news about what we were doing to get our city operational again. What they should be doing to stay safe or where we set up evacuation sites.

Are designated City public relations person was scripted to give reports to News on what we were doing on a regular basis when briefed by City Manager and her Department heads. Each department head was responsible for briefing public relations person on what departments were facing from our command post. This was quite a responsibility for our public relations person, and they had to polish their skills during drills. So if we ever had a disaster, they would be well polished. We explained that after the drill, all departments could use it when there was a need for it. Then we suggested we could keep it at our station three as they would be used as newscasters during our drills or if we needed it to film a public relations film for our city.

I also suggested that the training crew could film anything the departments in the city needed as scheduled through fire department as we were on duty 24-7. We went out and priced equipment that city could afford, and we did it in the most cost-effective manner possible to meet the fire department as well as city's needs. We included more expensive equipment that would be more of what we really wanted to buy to get the job done right.

We presented it to city manager and city council at the council meeting, justifying just it as we stated it above. I used the briefing method presented in this book. When I got to the end and asked them if they had any questions, they asked me one question, and I was prepared for it. They asked, "Don't you think our city would be better off in long run if we got the better equipment?" I was ready for that, and we got the more expensive equipment and a little more for any unexpected expenses that we were not aware of. We could have made due, but because we researched it and presented it well, we got more because they knew we were known for only asking for what we needed and nothing more. Where there is a will, there is a way. Don't take no for an answer and prepare more and ask for no more than you need as presented in this book. Prior proper planning prevents piss-poor performance. You can do it just as I did; just get prepared and give them hell.

We talked about finding people who were good at doing something you need and get them into doing it. They will be happier, and you will be too. For example, the case below shows you how to do it.

We were always looking for better ways to do our job better. We needed someone good on the computer to organize our programs and pull information needed together to make good decisions. I couldn't be good at everything but smart enough to know we needed a good computer person. Jim Nance showed a big interest in computer programming, and he learned the computer so well at work doing programs for us to get information we needed. He eventually developed our computer program. Last I heard, he was setting up computer programs for other cities.

I hope you can see where we are going with this. We are training others in our chain of command and ourselves to work smarter not harder and save time so we can do more for our organization. Does this make us more valuable? I would think so. If I had anybody showing these traits, I would be watching them and getting them ready for more responsibilities and promotion.

Have your computer person set up charting systems for projects and goals and objectives. Keep them simple, info in info out. The computer can only help you if you put good information in it. It's not a decision maker; it just presents you with good information for you and your subordinates to make good decisions. Don't be a hit-and-miss. Write things down, and make sure you have some kind of system to recall it later. Don't just forget about things that maybe combined with other information to make dynamic changes in your programs.

You will always have to be multitasker. Make sure you prioritize your tasks so they will best serve you and your organization. Keep the cut-and-paste tool in your toolbox of management skills. This is taking information from several sources, bringing them together in one place where you can use information for decision making. You can also do long-range forecasting with this information. I am going to be covering these and more subjects in the last chapter of my book. You can expect to get more information on these subjects there.

Well, we have planned, made decisions, talked about budgeting, organized to carry out our plan, and used evaluation at every turn to make a change in small baby steps. We have really learned the importance of evaluation at every turn, correct?

Last I want to say, use your time wisely. If you have to travel, take work with you, and keep in contact with people at home. When I was going through officer's school, there were no written directions. The TAC Officers told you only one thing and that time is our enemy.

What do you think that means? Remember we were going to be leaders of men, and the answers to problems may not be clear, and it is up to us to evaluate them and put them into operational plans. So time is our enemy, a lesson well learned on my part. Take everything you have to do to graduate. Prioritize most point values, and work on them first. Things with fewer values; don't worry so much about them. They never taught that in officer's school, but you better leave with that idea entrenched in your mind. I learned that lesson first week of school. I hope these examples have shown you how important planning and organizing is to each one of you.

Let's move onto leadership, a very important part of this book.

CHAPTER 3

Leadership

YOUR LEADERSHIP STYLE can make or break you. First, you need to find out what you are all about. You can't help anyone until you can help yourself. You can start learning leadership skills anytime, but for them to be really helpful to you, you must be in a place where all your basic needs are met. Maslow's theory of basic needs include air we breathe, food we eat, and shelter. The next need is feeling of belonging in community and at work. Then in the self-actualization phase, you are sure of yourself and what your specific needs are. In self-actualization, a person can feel the need to lead or just be happy being a member of community or workforce. We cover this right here in the beginning so you can make a self-inspection of yourself and the needs of people around you. For example, shelter and food needs on East Coast and West Coast are different. West Coast, it is easy to find food and shelter. On East Coast during winter a West Coast person may have some trouble in this area.

If that person worked for you, make sure you help him or her with tips on how to survive winters because they can't worry about work until their basic needs are met. Remember, if your basic needs are pulled out from under us, we immediately revert back to the basic needs. We have to stabilize those needs before we can move back into the self-actualization phase. This is just a little bit of information that can start you on developing your leadership skills.

I found early in my career how important psychology and knowledge of behavioral theories were important to me to make choices in my leadership style. They shaped how I would treat individual people. I was a frontline supervisor in both the fire department and military when I started building my leadership skills. If I did something wrong, I learned by my own mistakes. I also learned to watch other people around me to see what mistakes they made and learned from those as well. I started my tool bag way back then, and I am still learning today and keeping my mind open to change and new ways of doing things.

These concepts did help me to learn myself and others and gave me the ability to have a solid foundation to choose a leadership style for me.

Another thing I learned is that we cannot treat all people the same. I know, as you should know, that some people need an autocratic leader for them to function. Nothing wrong with that, and it doesn't make them a bad person. They just need to see things in black and white, that is all. Thank God, we learned this because treating everyone alike may destroy our employees, both the free thinkers and people who need direct supervision. But don't get me wrong on this one. When you start moving up the ladder, you have to have more free thinkers around you.

If you study Machiavelli and great leaders who have used his methods, you start to see the same characteristics in leaders of today and the past. Those who are successful are delegators, which I will cover later. They surround themselves with successful people who will support them and get the job done. They pull together to meet the same goals and objectives. They keep abreast of world affairs and how they influence their organizations as well as domestic issues. They know how important planning and organizing is and why leading and evaluating play such an important part of atmosphere they work in.

An organization might look like this one. Businesses and governments organize like this also. An emergency system like FEMA Incident Command System is set up the same way:

- CEO
- Planning Operations Logistics Resources
- Department heads [five to seven]
- Divisions [five to seven]

Down to the workers. Theses movers and shakers never forget how important every person is to an organization. Leaders know that organizing like this is the key to their operation. Everyone knows their position and what they need to do.

As we develop our skills, we must look at the behavior of people and ourselves, mesh it all together, and come up with a recipe for success. In order to do this, we need to watch people both within and outside our organization. Never forget people we serve, and make it foremost in your mind. They deserve our service at the most cost-effective method possible. This is true in the business, government, and military levels.

We are leaders, and more times than not we won't get the money we need to get the job done as we planned. As long as you have justified your position during the budget phase, take what you get, reevaluate, and do the best you can do. Don't complain what good does it do.

I have found that there are still some dictatorship-type leaders out there, and they seem to never get very high in the organization because they don't trust people to do a good job without them. These people want every decision to go through them. They don't trust their advisors or the people who work for them.

A democratic leader will take time to develop the people around him or her and values their input. They care about their employees' needs, both at work and home. These people seem to go high in the organization. They want people to tell them how they really feel about things, and they want to make their people feel safe.

Which type of leader do you want to be? Be careful here; you might have to revert to autocratic leadership during emergency. Military and public safety have to do that while on battleground or police or fire operating scene. I have done both military and fire department. Decisions must be made very quickly, and you don't have time for input. It is important to do some kind of lessons learned after incident and allow your personnel to make suggestions, which can be put in everyone's tool bags for success.

I believe Peter Drucker's term "management by objectives" is a very good start to developing your leadership style. Like I did in past; don't take an entire management style and incorporate it into your organization. Look at everything out there, and start developing your own unique style of managing people and resources. Really, it's all about keeping things simple. Develop methods for you to save yourself time and energy. You need to do what I call "hitchhike" on others' ideas and make them better. Once again, we are looking outside ourselves and to others to make ourselves better.

First and foremost in my mind, I have always managed the someway I wanted to be treated. Early in my military and fire department career, I was introduced to hard dictatorships, even to the point that no comment was the best comment. Some thoughts there, I have found that anytime you are in a new position or are in a new atmosphere you haven't worked in, listen and watch to what is going on. If you just jump in and start making decisions, you will find opposition from personnel already there.

People don't like change, and they certainly don't like it done without their input. Let's cover this a little later. In both positions, military and fire service, I found the first six months were critical that you be under a very strict autocratic leader. Even to university graduates as they must be taught basics of job that just can't be learned during school. I say this here because some university graduates are hired in management positions in city, county, state, and federal government. Business does this all the time.

I feel every manager should learn every job of people they will be supervising as well as be introduced to the job right above his or hers. I will come back to some important things I mentioned here such as my feelings regarding new positions, university graduates, things that can't be learned in school, and learning the job below and above.

Going back to beginning of my career, I found that after the first six months I wanted to grow, but my supervisors didn't want that. I don't think they really did it on purpose; they did it because they were supervised that way and felt you must experience the same as they did.

I didn't like the way I was being treated, so I went to school and started learning fire science and management techniques. Of course, I wanted to share this with my supervisors and what do you think happened? They said shut up and keep your opinions to yourself. I believe I saw a revolution in city right through to federal governments. What I mean here, fire departments and military could run like this because they did not have to show profit and were not really held accountable for their budgets. As leaders in cities started becoming more educated, there was more planning, and citizens started requiring more bang for the buck. This required doing things different thus the end of doing things same way.

My main point here, I didn't like the way I was being treated in the organization, so I swore I would do something back then. When I finally did get in the position that I could change things, I made a lot of mistakes. I was young, and I had no problems with handling fires and mission of U.S. Navy assignments. I had problems with writing reports, doing personnel evaluations, and direct supervision.

Really, I didn't know what city was doing or fire department except our mission was to protect life and property and respond to emergency incidents. I don't think city manager or fire chief knew anymore than me. That scared me; I really could find no help. I went back to school and started taking classes out of fire science.

These included psychology and government as well as business management. I found in U.S. Navy they did help me to see whole picture during Vietnam War. I started to see how everything started fitting together and that it was a team effort. If we didn't do our job, people died. That makes you do the best you can possibly do and more. That is a lot of pressure on an eighteen-year-old, and I found I grew more in that two-year period than ever before or after. I can honestly say that the U.S. Navy developed me into the man I am today. The U.S. Air Force refined me and developed me to reach for my goals whatever they were. I highly recommend any one starting off to join the U.S. military serve our country and learn a job you will be happy in.

I studied Plato, Machiavelli, Geronimo, Apache Chief Magnus, and great military leaders and started forming a new leadership style based on them and behavioral science. A little about Geronimo here; he was a great warrior who was the grandson of a great chief. He was very smart, a good orator, and outstanding at planning attacks and escapes. He had poor people skills when it came to the Apache Tribe. He was for himself and used deceit to get what he wanted.

He felt all Mexican and white men should be killed for crimes against Apache. He tried to have Chief Mangos removed so he could be chief. Due to his dishonesty and poor people skills, he never became chief but commanded renegades. He died, a drunk at age seventy.

Mangos cared about his people and took that into consideration when ordering attacks on white men and Mexicans . . . Only doing it when the soldiers and settlers stole or attacked the Apache. He was considered a great chief who cared for his people and their living conditions.

He had great behavioral skills. Case in point, both were great leaders and the winner to lead. The Apache went to Mangos who had great people and leadership skills. I hope this makes you understand that great leaders must have good people skills too. I was impressed with the war strategies he used against white men and Mexicans. He would study his enemy, then do hit-and-run tactics like guerrilla warfare fighting. He could look at where he had to attack and planned out every detail of attack and escape. His raids were always successful and he had ability to attack and win where other leaders or warriors couldn't. That is why I read it in sixth grade and have read it again every five years. He was a fascinating warrior, and I recommend you read *Warrior of the Wolf Pack* by Moody.

I also tried to incorporate Peter Drucker as whole program. I had more success with my leadership and was able to use a more democratic system that enabled taking chances and letting my personnel grow, but that was not enough, so I just kept listening and learning and exposing myself to every opportunity that let me learn more and new things.

I hope you are starting to get it. It takes a lot to be a good leader, and you won't get it all here. Use this book to look into things and subjects I have talked about. Find yourself a mentor, and go to that person and ask for help. This person should cause you to be inspired.

Pick someone you want to be like and look up to. For me, that was Brig. Gen. Allen Boone and Brig. Gen. Eddie Aguirre, also Prof. Tom Bream, five-star Gen. Douglas McArthur and President Eisenhower, five-star admirals Chester Nimitz and Bull Hulsey.

One of my ideals is the father of our navy, John Paul Jones. When asked to surrender by the British captain who thought he was defeated, Jones replied, "I have not yet begun to fight. What have I told you I say when told I can't do something?"

It just makes me want to show them I can. When I was contracting a fire prevention program for the City of Imperial Beach Fire Department, I was inspecting there and The San Diego Port Authority Pier. I advised Fire Chief, David Ott, that we needed a new sprinkler system on pier, that we didn't have enough water for system, and it was hooked up wrong. Chief Ott and I wrote a report to San Diego Port Authority on the problem and my solution.

Remember, I told you never give me your problems, give me your solutions. Well, I practice what I preach, and I can walk the walk. Within a year, San Diego Port Authority did it. I showed how to do it cheaper as I engineered system to National Fire Protection Association Standards 21 and California Standards Title 19. If you know what you're doing, it's easy. Thanks to Chief Ott for letting me do that. Hope everything in Del Mar, California, is going good for you.

When I was in the sixth grade after my first reading of Geronimo, I knew I wanted a career in the military. They had the programs back then about West Point and Annapolis, and of course, I decided I wanted to go to the United States Military Academy at Annapolis.

I took all college prep classes at Rubidoux High School and joined The U.S. Navy Sea Cadets. I was fourteen when I joined and eighteen when I left. During that time, I became one of the top cadets in U.S. Navy Sea Cadets at the Norco Naval Surface Warfare Lab in Norco, California.

I was a member of their precise drill team known throughout Southern California for drilling precision and performance in parades from Indio to San Diego and Los Angeles and back to inland valley.

I went to Hawaii in 1966 and came back on USS *Sperry* a submarine tender based in San Diego that was about two-and-one-half-week cruise

EDWARD E. WEISS JR.

from Hawaii. I went on shakedown cruises with USS *England*, a guided missile frigate the USS *Long Beach*, a light cruiser, and USS *Higher*, our home ship. We were taught seamanship by officers and men.

My fellow students at Rubidoux High School nicknamed me Admiral Ernie as my middle name is Ernest. You see I had a big dream; I wanted to become a four-star admiral, and I wanted to be chief of naval operation, and I believe I would have made a good one. I even had Senator Tunney's of California approval for appointment.

Well, things happen, and I joined U.S. Navy as enlisted man. I ended up going to fire department and started on a career there. I loved the fire department, and helping people was something I have always loved to do. I stayed in reserve, which is another thing I loved. I switched to California Air National Guard, Fresno, home of the 144th Fighter Interceptor Wing in 1980 and was commissioned in 1982. I went to Officers School at Magee Tyson Air Force Base in Knoxville Tennessee where the 1982 World's Fair was held, and I met Senator Baker of Tennessee and Fernando Marcos, president of the Philippines.

I was in charge of the honor guard on the twenty-one gun salute to President Marcos. That was quite a day. My point here is, remember back in the first chapter I talked about life being a dartboard. You always shoot for 100 percent, but sometimes you only get 90, 80, or 70 percent. Well, I think I did pretty well in life. I shot for 100 percent of my initial goal. I had to reevaluate my plan take a few small steps, organize again, and lead right back on to the leaderboard where I started hitting home runs again.

This has happened to me many times in my life, but I keep getting back up and start going forward time after time. I want to thank all my military friends and associates as well as State of California Office of Emergency Services personnel and all city and government personnel I have met along the way. Special thanks to City of Clovis, California, and one-time Mayor, Harry Armstrong.

So find people and theories you can study and find a present-day mentor. I told you sometimes I set my goals high. I would like to meet and have retired senator and World War II veteran, Bob Doyle, and his wife as my mentor in today's world. I really look up to them and believe they are true Americans.

I idealized President Regan and wife Nancy and his policies with our military. I thought President Bush and Barbra were what marriage is all about in our great nation, and I look up to him for decisions he made during First Gulf War.

I have studied every president of the United States since Kennedy. I have learned something from every one of them. They all are great leaders, democrat or republican it makes no difference. I have served each one of them since Nixon. I took an oath to protect the president of the United States and our great country from all threats both foreign and domestic and will to the day I die.

This book is my attempt to give back to local through federal governments as well as U.S. military and business what I have learned. If I make a difference in one person's life I will be happy. Who knows, maybe that person will influence somebody who invents something that saves a lot of lives. I have always thought that way, and I hope all of you will too. Let's pull together and make a difference in this world. America loves winners and hates losers. Let's get back to being economically solid with a strong military.

I remember I was in Japan in July 1969 when we first landed on the moon. I didn't even know about it as we just came out of Vietnam and a young Japanese dockworker in Sasebo, Japan, came running at me and kept saying, "Hey, Joe, America is number one." That felt good because we were number one then, and now the rest of the world just doesn't know it yet.

Treat people well, and they will treat you good. As a young supervisor every time I tried to do something, I ran in to men at the time who tried to take advantage of me, and I would have to slam hammer on them. I stopped really, trying to change from a dictatorial leader to a democratic leader until after I went outside fire science.

I found I had thirst for knowledge once I started learning about Machiavelli, behavioral theories, and great leaders in military and government. This actually started in sixth grade when I read Geronimo, and I wanted to be as tough as him and learn his methods on fighting—hit and run, hit and run until you wear the enemy down.

Now you can see why when I was introduced to Machiavelli's *Art of War*, I started using those leadership characteristics. I never mentioned that before, but I do it for my military and business leaders; they know what I mean. Police departments know what I mean here too. I know for sure, my good friend, and as I type this, I am smiling. Police Chief Gunner Galvin does. That's at least Lt. Col. Jerry Galvin, United States Marine Corps Reserve Ret. and a Second Lieutenant in Vietnam. I lost touch with Jerry before First Gulf War, but I bet he got another National Defense Medal as I did. Police Chief, Jerry Galvin, called the "Fix it Police Chief," was my friend, and military leader as well. Last I heard, he was in Mendota,

California so he could be near his grandchildren. Good luck, Jerry, to you and your grandchildren. Thanks for your friendship and service to our country. Welcome home from Vietnam, Jerry, and to all Vietnam veterans, I say welcome home. But not just them to the greatest generation of World War II like Senator Bob Doyle, a man I really would like to meet, and here are stories about then and now.

Let's get back to new positions. Sometimes we feel like we want to jump in with both feet but don't do it. Give everything you do time to digest before you start making decisions that can upset the whole applecart. Remember, there are times you will have to do just that. Public safety emergencies are one of them, and we know what to do right. Do what we have to do, but get back to personnel and do lessons learned. Reevaluate what happened and set new plans in operation, right? Right, that's what we do but not here in this one. Here we look, listen, and feel what's going on before we do anything. Go to your top employee or chief navy sergeant all other branches.

Be careful what you call them; make sure you address them right. One wrong move makes everything wrong. I addressed a Marine master sergeant as a sergeant major, and it ruined the mood. Oh well, be careful both in business, government, and military. Get all the information before you make any decisions. Don't change a thing until it needs changing, and never ever change just to change. If you need to change, assemble your people together, again assemble what problems are, and find out what facts are, possibilities, probabilities own situation is, make a decision, set your plan of operation, set up periodic evaluations. Keep your personnel in loop and make sure they do the same for you. Mostly, everybody is happy now. Wasn't that easy? I think we are learning something here that can help us the rest of our lives.

How about those university graduates, I believe are going to college for four years and earning degree in discipline does insure they are organized and well equipped to do a job in lower management depending on the job. It has been found that in more specific jobs such as police, fire, and public works everyone degree or not must learn basics and move up ladder. That degree will prepare them better for upper levels, but they will have to pass test like everyone else.

The degrees are good for engineers, planning, finance, operations, aids, and so forth. Lawyers, doctors, and nurses definitely get extra consideration especially in military where they only spend a few weeks in officer's school where they are taught how military does things.

I want to say it right here that for military, this book is only food for thought. Your bread is buttered in professional military school of which there are a lot of requirements. I recommend you do them early and go to in-house professional schools not correspondence when you can.

I want to cover employee evaluations here. First, make sure you are communicating with your employee first. Never evaluate an employee without setting up program of responsibilities he or she shall meet during quarters throughout the year for best results. If you have done your job, this will be easy, and you don't have to make up things for evaluations.

Now we should have already set up programs for our employees because first of all, we kept them involved. They know where our organization is going and where they fit in, right? Right, we included them in all that. We started evaluating goals and objectives, and they committed to doing certain things to make sure they are met and if not to set up emergency meeting with you to make small changes where necessary. Also you have told them you will be looking at the plan at set times that are scheduled by you to check. Well, they know what's expected of them, so let's let them fill out the evaluation.

You say what that will never work. Well, give it a chance; they will be their own worst enemy. That way, you don't have to bring up weak points because that is negative. If we are going to motivate our personnel, we will use a few behavioral theories here because we want our people motivated. Just pick out four areas you want to evaluate them on; rate them in those areas and always do comments. Never leave them blank; do overall rating. Then give them areas to comment on anything they may want to comment on how to do things better. I call this my management by objectives evaluations, and it's here for you to use if you like. Adapt it to your set evaluations by organization because this works. I have found it makes bad employees satisfactory and good employees excellent and outstanding.

We are here to motivate our personnel and nothing does me better than to see one of my employees promote over me because I have done my job. Was that simple? I think so, now where else can we save time? If I left something out, I hope I catch it later, but I think you got the idea.

Discipline should now be easy. If it has to be done, do it and make it simple. First, tell him or her he/she did wrong, no time for them to talk here. Tell them that they are better than that, and you expected better of them. Ask them to write a small report on what they think went wrong and how they will correct their problem. It's not your problem; they did it. Put it back on them. That's teaching them to be responsible, and never

EDWARD E. WEISS JR.

take any crap from them like "I am not a supervisor. You do it." If they are really persistent about this, come down hard; if you do it, but be short and to point.

They will never give you that crap again, and others will hear about it too. Put a copy in the files. Make one for you and one for them, and make sure they sign it along with what they will do to correct the problem. Make sure the copy goes to the personnel. Remember, it is not our job to catch them doing things wrong; we want to see them doing good and make comment on it then. Don't make this a habit. Let them know when they have really impressed you and make sure then you write comments on that and put in files like personnel too with a copy to your employee.

When disciplining, make sure you talk to them so it's documented right if you do have to fire someone. When employees do good, make sure you put that in their evaluations too. Make sure it is definitely in overall performance for year. Remember this tool is to motivate your employees and improve their overall performance at work. Never get into personal business but offer to talk at their call.

Keep an open-door policy and let them know it, and keep door open when you're not working on things that require your concentration or quite time like talking on phone. I always kept an open-door policy, and employees knew when door was closed, I was busy. They would have to e-mail me or leave massage with my secretary or clerk.

If someone else could answer questions, they knew where to go. I would never answer simple questions for them. I wasn't a dictionary or encyclopedia. I would tell them where to find answers and come back and tell me what it was that they found out. They learned things better, and they didn't bother me for every little small thing. It also gave me an opportunity to find out what real problems in organization are. Remember, never try to get informants or be one. If I found someone to be an informant, I knew I couldn't trust them, and I hate tattletales who like to cause trouble. I make it my business to get rid of them. Trust people like I have been preaching. The bad people in your organization will be caught by you or your employees who will have your back.

CHAPTER 4

Evaluation

WELL, I AM happy to be here because I have evaluated my book up to this point, and I hope you have been evaluating yourself and your programs at work as well. By now, I hope that you are finding that this book is for free thinkers and people who are looking to take the road less traveled. Most leaders that won't let go have stopped reading this book by now, but I hope not. They still need the basics I have presented for you, but they will believe that giving personnel around them trust won't work in their situation. Maybe they are right, but I think not. Jobs that need this type supervision are high risk and brand-new employees. Other than that, I hold to the fact that you need good people around you to succeed at work and in your personal life, and the only way to get them is developing them through the ways suggested in this book.

Before we go any further, I want to talk about mission statements and evaluating them. A mission statement is simply no more than one paragraph that communicates what the organization is designated to accomplish by what the board members in business, city council in cities, and government by executive and legislative branches. The above people set where we are going and give us direction in what services will needed to get there.

As managers, it's our job to take their direction and monies allocated to do it in the most cost-efficient and effective manner possible. We have a responsibility to them, and the citizens they represent to do this to the best of our ability using managing techniques we have learned. It is quite an honor to be in a position like that, and we should accomplish it, do it with that in mind.

To do this, we will have to plan, organize, lead, and evaluate getting the input of others and finally have it approved by those who govern us before we proceed further. Then we set our mission statement to accomplish what they have approved which is our plan of operation and set objectives small mission statements for man power and resources to accomplish. Quite a job, isn't it? Slow down and think about it. How do you eat an elephant? One bite at a time. Break it all down, and delegate your responsibilities and start working. The CEO, president, governor, city manager can't do it by themselves. They must have people they trust around them to recommended, and do the same in the areas they represent and responsible for . . . It's like in a big organizational chart because that's what it is. These responsibilities are filtered all the way down to the frontline supervisors and mid-managers. Can you see where you fit in and how important your job is and those beneath you? You have been given quite an honor and responsibility that you need to take to heart in everything you do.

A mission statement should answer the five Ws: who, what, where, when, why, and how. You take what you have been entrusted to do, and write your statement out taking into consideration your resources and man power given to accomplish this mission.

Let's take a city fire department, for example, and get tight into the meat of this whole thing.

It is the mission of the city fire department to protect the citizens and property of city by providing fire protection and other related emergency services to the citizens of city in the most efferent, effective and effective manner possible. The fire department will do this by forming and utilizing programs to include but not limited to fire prevention, hazardous material containment and confinement, emergency medical services, heavy rescue, and all other related services to the citizens in the most cost-efficient and effective manner possible. This will be done by utilizing all of its resources, man and equipment. Let's see if we answered five Ws? Who are the city citizens and fire department. ? What were going to provide services necessary to do this? When are we going do that and that is now. Where in the city? Why because the city and council assigned it to us, and it's our job to do it. How by providing our service in the most efficient and effective manner using man power resources given to us.

Objects are short sentences one or two on how you are going to meet the mission. Each area I mentioned such as fire prevention, fire department, and the others should have separate mini mission statements that support overall mission of the fire department. I will write some objectives as examples for fire prevention.

Objectives

1. Prevent fire in the city by providing fire prevention program using the required standards as set forth by the state of California and the National Fire Protection Association
2. Educate people why prevention inspections inside their places of work are necessary to prevent fires
3. Engineer or problem solve every violation you find in building by showing them how violations can be corrected in a cost-effective manner
4. Enforce fire prevention violations in the city when necessary by issuing fines
5. Perform plan checking for buildings, fire sprinkler systems, and site maps for new construction in residential and business sites providing any requirements and comments to contractors in a timely manner

By writing your objectives, you can see how when finished, you can organize fire prevention program into smaller areas of responsibility with even more specific objectives. When we are finished, we have an entire fire prevention program that supports the mission statement, goal of fire department. Now we can plan, organize, lead, and evaluate to get it up and running properly.

After each program is done the same, you have a fire department that can meet its mission statements by accomplishing the objectives set by each program with in it, and we have built a fire department that is both efficient and effective. As each department in city does this along with the city manager's mission statement, we have built an entire city. Now you have an operating city, and it can be put in an organization chart that shows it support and services for city council, citizens, employees to see how the city is organized and operated to provide an outstanding service to its citizens and business owners. That wasn't hard, was it? I hope you now have more understanding of where you fit in organization and your importance to its serving. When setting up your area of responsibility, you should set your area of responsibility up like I have done below and write your objectives out. Now you have a plan that has to be evaluated and changed when necessary with small baby steps to guide everything into place for optimal results. Will your area of responsibility be satisfactory just to get minimum standards accomplished or outstanding? I want to be outstanding, and if I fall short somewhat at least I am above average and stay above it at all times. It's like the Bart board of life. Shoot for bull's eye each time, and if you only get 90 percent, it's better than failing.

Keep your people involved in this entire process as suggested in this book, and your job will be easier in doing this entire project.

I put this here to show you where you fit into an organization and how it is very important to be continually evaluating your plan at every step you make. Once we have this plan in operation, we must test it at least yearly to ensure it is at least meeting goals and objectives determined to operate an organization and shall we say divisions within it.

If you remember, the USAF does this by sending minimum requirements to units that must be met, and then it's up to that unit to develop the program further to receive an outstanding operational readiness inspection rating. Cities and other government entities should be doing this as well. You can test your plan to see if it is meeting your standards as set forth by its governing body by having a disaster drill with scenarios given to departments to show their ability to perform the goals and objectives as determined by CEO, department of defense, state, county, and city.

If the USAF believes it's important for a base to be rated on its ability to operate by having inspector general inspection teams devoted to nothing but this. It's that important to the U.S. Air Force to evaluate every aspect of a unit from administration and every operation it does to perform the mission. It's important to evaluate and make small changes when necessary to reach your goal. It would be advantageous for a city to test and evaluate its ability to perform at minimum standards.

Evaluation is very important to do, and you must be evaluating the right thing to be efficient and effective. After each evaluation of an organization's ability to operate and perform, there should be evaluations done like lessons learned and incorporate them into your plan as necessary. Keep the planning circle moving because to do it right, it never ends and always will be showing you where to make direction changes. Keep them small; that must be made to provide you with an outstanding business or organization that is doing what it said it could do even better. We don't accept satisfactory as an option, do we?

Evaluation is just as important as planning

You are doing all those things to start moving the organization and area you are responsible for in the right direction. To be able to claim this, you and your employees will have to do close inspections of the programs they are responsible for, and you need to ensure all these programs fit together to produce the results you are looking for.

We talked about the difference between being efficient and being effective. This is where the cow eats the cabbage, and you have to be able to walk the walk. If you have read any books on successful salespeople they emphasize always keep closing. They have to be able to close, or they get no money. They are keeping their pipeline open. Definition pipeline is deals salesman has in process from start to finish. Even a salesman has to do all the things we have been talking about and more. Well, salespeople must keep doing the right thing right, or they won't close deals.

You can be efficient at doing the wrong things, and you have to be careful when setting up your plan, which takes a lot of time, and organizing yourself and others to meet the goals and objectives you have set and believe are important to them, you, and the organization as a whole. Now you have planned and organized, and you start leading people and resources to accomplish everything that you have accomplished. You feel like a conductor of a band, and you are happy to see how everything you have planned and organized for is coming together as you lead your people to success. You have been evaluating all this time too. Everything looks good, and one day your supervisor comes down and says everything you are doing here looks well, but it isn't fitting into his/her overall operation. He/she gives you some direction and asks you to fix it. Well, you were being efficient but not effective.

Well, you better find out how to do the right thing right. Maybe this was your first time out, and you made a mistake. Right now, you don't look very good to your superiors and employees as well as others in the organization. Well, you did everything you learned here, but when you got to all the areas about evaluation, you skipped over those sections of reading because you didn't give it a high rating in your limited estimation. Now is evaluation just as important as planning, organizing, and leading? I hope you believe that it is because now we have to start working from worse position than from scratch to fix this whole thing.

Are you just going to give up or put your thinking hat on right now and say to yourself right that there is something to be said about doing the right thing right? From this point forward, you swear you will never make this mistake again. You will ensure you are being efficient and effective and know the difference. This time you were lucky and your supervisor caught the problem; next time, you better have red flags in place to jump up if you are moving in the wrong direction.

Well, it's time to send damage control out, get a report back, and start shoring up so we can meet the next challenge. Well, we just set another plan into operation and remember this time the importance of the seven Ps: Prior proper planning prevents piss-poor performance. That term stings right now, doesn't it? Well, let's saddle up and do this again. First of all, look at the entire situation and don't get tunnel vision here. Go back and get facts, probabilities, possibilities, probabilities, own situation, and make a decision. Put it into operation and keep evaluating.

You may be surprised here and find that everything is not lost. Remember I said never make big changes, always take baby steps when changing. If that change works, keep going if not evaluate again and make small change again. You will find that if you make a big change in your plan, if you go wrong, it will take twice as long to get back to the original place of change.

Well, let's get back and start utilizing your employees here early on, be up front with them. They are human and will understand. Nine chances out of ten, they will have ideas about what needs to be done to turn things around. Go to your supervisor now, and keep him/her up to date. Remember you should have run this by him in first place. Maybe that is where we went wrong, but regardless now we are fixing our mistake. I am going to revisit all of the steps I took to get where I am at this point, keep my employees informed, and meet regularly with them to evaluate everything I am doing. Yes, it is slowing me down at this point, and I am rebuilding to make things stronger. Just like broken bones are stronger once they break and mend. The part of organization your responsible for will be stronger for this mistake if you take all the necessary steps to right your wrong. That which does not kill me only makes me stronger. As we go along in life, we will become stronger and stronger every day of our lives. When you stop learning, you are dead.

So now we look at our plan; is there something we missed? Address it now again, ask your personnel what they think is right and when you start coming up with some ideas about proceeding. Go to your supervisor and include him or her too. If everything looks good, start proceeding forward with new goals and objectives. Again involve your people here and get important feedback from them. If they are a part of your plan, they will not want to fail anymore than you do. When you have really developed your employees, they are going to go the extra mile for you, and you should do the same for them. I have found that in later years, a lot of my close associates turned out to be good friends in the long run. It's kind of like love if they leave during the hard times they were never your friends to begin with. In the military, they say love is like a bird; if you let it go and it never comes back, it was never yours to begin with. Friends can be like that too. If you look back over the years, they were always for themselves and were not interested in you just what they could get like favors and so on. Life in general is like this; when you find a good friend, stick by him/her through thick and thin.

So we have done our planning and see what changes if any you have to make in your organization and what you have to do to fix it. Hopefully, you don't have to change much. Do not change if you don't need to. If it's not broken, don't fix it. A little preventative medicine goes along was here. The only organizing you should have to do here is organizing your resources to accomplish the new goals and objectives that may have to be set. If not, you have a big job ahead, take your time, get everyone involved both up and down the ladder of your organization. Set up evaluations and red flags that can set you back in the right direction in case you start to regress in the wrong direction. Evaluations are important in the evaluation phase especially if you have to make a change again. Once you and your personnel have found what you need to change, change it slowly.

Remember what happens if you make big changes fast. People in your organization will not like the change and wonder why there is so much change. They start to lose confidence in you and organization. This causes them to be less motivated. If we have studied behavioral science, we will see that what we are doing in an organization will make them more inverted, worrying about their own good. There is less work getting done, and people will be afraid to stick there neck out for anyone. Keep your changes small and take baby steps when putting everything into operation, and your personnel will not feel threatened and will work with you, not against. This makes your job easier, and it also keeps them involved.

Well, we have been planning, organizing, and leading to correct problems in an organization and make changes only when necessary. Have your personnel go latterly to make sure every angle of problem has been addressed. You also need to do this and find out if they will be getting information they need from you to operate. Once you have that set up, start meeting with your boss and show him/her what you are doing and get commitment from him/her to review your programs at least every quarter. This is one way we will stop any problems from coming back or new ones from popping up. Next, set up meetings with your employees to review their progress and programs and keep on schedule as well as look for any

EDWARD E. WEISS JR.

defects or new problems that appear in their area of operations. Jump on them right away before they become a big problem. At this point, we are using preventative measures to right everything that went wrong. Stay the course on this one and your back in operation again. Hopefully you never get to this place, but if you do we have went over how to fix it.

I hope you have now figured out that this process never, ever stops. You are always going to be following through on every thing your organization does and every thing your part of organization does whether you stay at level you are at or move up the ladder. The process never changes, and your personnel just get better at it. Be invocating and lead by example. Keep yourself open to change, never get tunnel and think outside the box sometimes. Don't be afraid to take risks, but keep everyone informed when doing so. Plan to win and you will as long as you include the basics of what you have learned in this book. Personnel around you are your best allies. Keep them informed, and they will do the same for you.

Evaluating is a very important part of planning; think of it as interconnecting. Once one process is done, the next starts until you are back to planning. For example, planning, organizing, leading, and evaluating. It never stops; it just keeps repeating itself. That is the planning circle. This is where evaluation is very important because you have to start looking outside your organization to meet change in environment you function in. Make sure you do some forecasting so the organization can be ready to meet its mission now and in the future.

It is very important for you to realize that you and your personnel must be a recipe for change, and it must be incorporated in the process we have been learning about. Planning, organizing, leading, and evaluating done in a continuous manner must ensure that you are taking into consideration change in world, national, and local affairs. This change will affect your organization and the way you do things. Allow for it in evaluation step, and don't forget about it. Make sure you check other departments in your organization to make sure what you are doing won't adversely affect another department. For example, a city where you have a city manager and department heads in fire, police, planning, finance, public works, and other appropriate departments. The entire department heads meet with city manager on weekly basis to ensure everybody is on same page and going forward to meet the mission of the city.

In the above example, the planning department is doing a lot of talking to each department head as to growth of city and changing environments that will have to be addressed. The long-range forecasting done here is not set in stone, and before it comes about many changes in city will occur as well as plan to meet new progress. This process never stops, and you can't let it stop in your area. Be ready for a challenge for now and in the future. I believe we are ready to do this. Now we will move into the summary chapter where I will retell you what I have already told you and add more definition where I deem necessary. I can tell you right now one of them will be forecasting as I don't believe I did that justice.

Try new things, and don't be afraid of mistakes. Know where you are going, involve your people, and always be developing them, and keep evaluating things. See you in chapter five.

CHAPTER 5

Summary

WE HAVE LEARNED a lot of things, and it is time to review them and make sure we have gotten every point and idea. When we think about management, it is paramount that we know the best managers are going to be the ones who have good people skills and have taken the time to dive deep into behavioral science and study what makes people tick. As I hope you all remember, I told you Professor Bream from California State University, Fresno, took a liking to me an took upon himself to develop my management skills.

If it hadn't of been for Professor Bream, I don't think my leadership style would have the depth that it had in past and today. I am still learning something every day about behavioral science and managing people. During this chapter's writing, I am sitting in the lounge of billeting quarters Camp Pendleton Marine Corps Base, Oceanside, California. It is July 3, 2010, the day before our great country's birthday.

During the last couple of days, I have heard some very interesting analogies of how young Marines feel about what they are doing in regards to national and world affairs. I am not in the Marines, but they can identify with me because of my U.S. Navy and U.S. Air Force affiliation. At first when I identify who I am, they are very intimidated. It doesn't take long to get them feeling comfortable with me, and the first thing they say to me is thank you for caring. You see right there; they are looking to be recognized as Marines, and once I reinforce to them that they should be proud of who they are and what they do, I can see a sparkle in their eye. Now I would never talk to them when they or I are on a United States Military Base or installation as I am not in their chain of command.

These young men and women who could not get home this Fourth of July are all over Southern California, looking for enjoyment and a good safe time. What I am really getting at here is if the average citizen or I give them the consideration due to them and really listen to what they have to say and give them a chance to express their feelings, you will start to see them stick their chests out more. It is the same with your employees; if you show them you care, they will be more open to you. Now it is up to you to develop your personnel into valued employees.

I was talking to a young Marine Corps PFC who told me about a young Marine who was having problems in training and felt bad about himself. I found he was an outstanding marksman. He told me the sergeant started treating him better overall, and the young man became the best in his class and started helping others. This is a true story from yesterday. Lesson here is if you catch people doing things right and praise them when they are doing well, they will automatically start improving. Their weak areas will become satisfactory, and they become outstanding employees overall. Everybody is good at something, and it is our job as supervisors to find and develop it. My eyes were big when the PFC told me this story, and even after I explained what happened to that bad trainee he still didn't comprehend what I was saying, but I believe someday he will.

As you can see, it is important for every manager to take time with his or her personnel and find out what their needs are and make sure we get them met to the best of our ability. Another priority is to always know the pulse of the citizens or what you need to produce to meet their needs. That's in business, government, and military. We need to be talking with them, meeting Joe Blow citizen on the street, listening to their needs and wants. Then come up with a plan that is intended to give them the most bang for their buck. We may not be able to meet all their needs, but we must make a decision and set a plan of operation to be efficient and effective. During my time in the fire service, U.S. military or business I always made it my most important responsibility to protect and serve the public. I liked giving of myself and the things I learned about people by just helping them. After I had helped someone through a really rough time is when I felt best about myself and the job I was doing. In military and fire service if we had a bad day, people died. That was not an option, so we could not let bad days affect our ability to function. Thank God, we have people who do this for a living and face it each and every day. I thank you for carrying on.

So now we have utilized our personnel to help us plan, and we are developing their abilities to improve in job performance every day. They are an important part of our operation, and they will help you to organize for best results. Last of all but not least of all, they and we will evaluate and make small changes in a plan to meet changes in the organization. They and you will meet at least quarterly on established programs, weekly on new programs, and monthly on programs going from beginning stage to well established. You will also make planning, organizing, leading, and evaluation an everlasting thing. When one area starts, another area begins, and you just keep going through each step to refine your operation.

Next I would like to give you an example of a large plan for emergencies in state of California such as earthquakes, fires, and floods. In this example, the U.S. Air Force, reserves, and California Air National Guard worked with personnel from the California Office of Emergency Services to prepare a workable plan to move personnel and resources into a disaster area rapidly. The personnel who went into the disaster zone were there to rescue people and medically treat victims injured during, for example, an earthquake. We could then move people, injured patients, and equipment to designated areas and hospitals for treatment of injuries received during disaster or after.

As you can see, this is quite a tasking. We had three representatives from the northern, central, and southern part of the state. I was the representative from the central state. The U.S. military met with the California Office of Emergency Services to come up with this plan and tasking of our men and women and other resources in undertaking such a monumental plan of operation. I was always thinking prior proper planning prevents piss-poor performance through the process and looked to subordinates for ideas . . .

We started meeting in mid-1980s to come up with this plan. First, we covered the basis of the objectives of our mission plan as that was pretty obvious. We wrote the mission statement out and worked as a group and individually to come up with our objectives, which were first to move personnel and equipment into an area and then move injured out while still maintaining the flow of personnel and resources into area if demands increased. We designated three areas to work out of: March Reserve Air Force Base Riverside, California, Fresno, Air National Guard Base at Fresno International AirPort, and Sacramento at Bealle Air Force Base.

If the incident occurred in Southern California, Northern and Central California collected resources and personnel to send into March Air Force Base who distributed the resources and personnel to areas which needed help. March Air Force Base would receive helicopters to transport equipment and personnel to disaster areas if roads were down. The injured were transported back to March Air Force Base where they would be sent out on military aircraft to the central and northern part of state from there they were transported to local hospitals. This tasking called for working with medical professionals, governments, business contractors who supplied heavy and light equipment, food contractors and vendors, public safety, service organizations such as Red Cross, and host of smaller contractors like toilets and etc. I think you get the picture. It's a big tasking, and we had to get it into operation quickly, or people were going to die. We organized and reorganized. We led our personnel and resources, and just as important evaluated at every step of plan. Don't think this incident or plan did not change and change rapidly. Because it did before operation and during, and that is why we utilized the federal incident command system under a unified command. One boss being advised by other specialists such as U.S. Air Force resources, medical, public safety, Red Cross, to name a few.

This is quite an organization that must be in place and tested all the time to see if tasking was meeting the needs of people and state of California. See how a small committee got big real quick after we identified the squares to be filed. Remember who, what, why, where, when, and how rule really has to be answered here, so people know what's expected of them. I was honored to sit on that committee, and as you must know, things have changed as we have better resources, but basic plan and objectives still remains the same. Remember here, don't make big changes; it will screw you, personnel, and program up. Make small changes and watch for positive results. Again trust your people, develop their interests, and train them to make decisions, and bring you solutions to problems. Get rid of time wasters by developing their potential and teach them to solve own problems and bring you solution you and he or she can work with. Once again I have given you an example of how to make a decision. I hope you are ready to go on your own in this area.

Let's revisit employee evaluations here again. Do what I call management by objective evaluations where the employee already knows the criteria he or she is to be evaluated on. Have employees sit down with you and go over what they agreed to do. Have them fill evaluation criteria out on themselves and together and you both agree here whether results or objectives are being met. They will be harder on themselves than you ever would be, but don't allow them to give themselves bad evaluation if it is not warranted. If you have been doing your job, the evaluation will be good because you have been having short meetings with them to make sure they are meeting their own objectives, and you are giving them quarterly evaluations, right?

You are also always trying to catch them doing things right and letting them know what they did right as soon after it happens as possible. We are now really developing our employees to be happy employees who function pretty much on their own so we have more time to do forecasting and long-range planning. Remember, you will still need their help when doing that kind of planning. Keep them involved in all your activities as they are our best resources.

You too must be a motivated leader and manager to keep them motivated. Be continually teaching them and developing their skills. Always remember, you don't just hire motivated people; they have to be taught by you. It's your responsibility to teach them how to best serve the organization and your area of responsibility. You have to take the time in the beginning to do this, but once it's done, they and you will have an outstanding foundation to work from. It doesn't stop there; they and you have to keep evaluating and take small baby steps when some change is necessary. Teach them to be outstanding and motivated leaders. Be willing to take the time in the beginning to build you and those strong foundations for leadership and management. Go to behavioral science and learn it inside out, and you will be surprised what it can do for your leadership style. Get a mentor for yourself both present and past that you would like to be like read all you can about them and how they did it as well as meet with your mentor as often as possible. Look to past philosophers for their thoughts and theories, and see if you can identify with them like Machiavelli and so forth as I have chosen.

Look at leadership styles like Peter Drucker's Management by Objectives. Also I believe if you read this book first and then *The One Minute Manager,* you will be ready to start developing your own leadership style that works for you. Take parts of programs, mismatch or cut and paste them together. Massage them and put it to work for you. Don't ever forget no matter what program or style you choose, people are your most important resource, and you will need them to get anything accomplished. It is your job to develop them, so get busy. I hope this book has helped you and will be a part of your management and leadership bag of tools. I will be happy if this book helps you as it has helped me. Remember knowledge is power. Do you want to be a participant or a mover and shaker in your organization?

I am sitting here with Jack Sigman with the United States Marine Corps who received shrapnel from an RPG round while in Ramada, Iraq. He lost his right leg above the knee from the blast sustained while on quick reaction force supporting an Explosive Ordnance Disposal Team in his area of operation. I saw him and asked what happened and he told me and it is a motivational story that I believe he should be recognized for. They did a ground medevac on him to altacqadeum Iraq to an all services shock trauma unit. He can't remember what happened; he just knew he went there. He wanted to emphasize that the U.S. Navy Corpsman saved his life initially. He felt he was going to lose his legs and heard the surgeon talking about him. They took his leg off their. He was in a drug-induced coma, and they took him through Ramstad Germany and on to Bathsheba Naval Hospital. He was in a drug-induced coma this entire time.

While at Bathsheba, he received follow-on surgeries and cleaning out of wound. He started physical therapy there. The commandant of the Marine Corps was a regular visitor there, and Jack asked if he could stay in the Marines, and he told him he would see what he could do. The commandant told him to read all of the rules and regulation requirements governing the fitness of service members. Jack was wounded in mid-October, and he had a good fitted prosthetic leg by mid-December.

Nine months from the day he was wounded, he started working various jobs to work a regular schedule for the Marine Corps. His new assignment was training new Marines at Quantico, Virginia.

He spent four years at Quantico and is now stationed at Camp Pendleton Marine Corps Base. He is about to be assigned to the school of infantry where he will be an instructor training new Marines. He still has ten days, and that again is where I met him. He has three years to go and plans to start a small business under the Veterans Administration Act to be a certified services disabled small business owner. Like Jack says, he has a full-time job to worry about now. After that, he will worry about a business. When he does retire, he plans on doing general contracting and program management of infantry weapons and military contracting. This man really represents what the father of our navy, John Paul Jones, was all about when he said, "I have not yet begun to fight when faced with defeat."

I identify with Jack, and his story has inspired me to do better. Jack won't take no for an answer, and I wish him well in his future Marine Corps career and his business as a government contractor later on. Thank God, we have men like him to keep us going. That is why I get up every morning and look in the mirror and smile, saying someone out there will need me today; well, Jack, I needed you today.

I also had the opportunity *to speak with* Lucy or Luz Lopez a young female Marine who is deploying to Afghanistan on a public relations mission to help the Afghanistan receive medical aid and information on how to build schools etc. She was abandoned at age six and was adopted when she was twelve years old by wonderful parents who have clearly changed her life.

EDWARD E. WEISS JR.

I found her to be quite an intelligent person embarking on a great career with the Marine Corps. She is excited about being a Marine and has a lot to offer our great country. She is an ambitious Marine who wants to learn their language and identify with female Afghans. When she comes back, she wants to qualify for Officers school. I believe she would make an outstanding officer candidate after talking to her. I know she has found a family in her adoptive parents and in the Marine Corps as well, and I would love to be at her graduation after completing officer's school. A quick note, she is training with fifty-four other female Marines who will also deploy with her. Good luck to all of them and the Marine Corps on this great endeavor for mankind. Thank you, Lucy, you too have inspired me today.

I know this is my summary, but I believe those stories warranted mention on how things change our lives. We can be ruined by them or fight on to better ourselves and the people we touch. Keep praising your personnel to carry on like the two stories I have chosen to share with you.

Next, let's talk more about some of the terms I have used in this book. Life is like a dartboard; always shoot for 100 percent, and if you only get 90 or 80 percent, that's good too. At that point, reevaluate and polish what you came up with. Then move on and take other shots at different goals and objectives. Don't gild the lily.

Remember that I have found that 20 percent of my work produced 80 percent of my yield. Polish that a little and go on. Don't waste your time spending 80 percent of your work perfecting it. I have found time and time again that by the time I did that, things had changed, and it wasn't that important. Move on to your next project. If you teach yourself and your personnel this, there will less time spent on protecting what maybe unimportant later and more time spent on planning and forecasting for the future. If it is that important, you will determine it later, and you may have a better idea on how to prefect it.

I have found that if I start running into problems, if I just stop and come back to it later I will have a better idea. Some of my best ideas have come in the middle of the night. Keep a notepad and write them down, or you might forget something that will be really helpful to you and your organization. Never be afraid to talk to people. Listen to what they have to say and act on it. If they have a good idea, never claim it as your own. Let them share in the glory, and they will in turn share more with you. Like the shark in the tuna tank, make them swim better and up their oxygen level so that they live more. The shark only ate enough to satisfy its hunger. Who would ever have believed that one?

Think about your time wasters and teach them how to solve their own problems. Bring me your solutions not your problems. Then the both of you can determine how to solve them. Remember to always be catching people doing the right thing. This will motivate them even more, and they will be display this trait time and time again. We like to be praised and our personnel do too. When you see them doing good things, tell them right away. We are all salesmen in life. Always keep closing deals by selling yourself. This is true for lawyers, businessmen, military personnel, and members of local governments as well as federal employees. If you don't do it, no one will. It's up to you to make things happen in your life.

Think about behavioral science and political theorists who have shaped leadership styles. You have to read them and come up with your own ideas on how to lead. Communication will be one of your best assets if you do it and your worst if you don't keep everyone informed both up the ladder and down it. Don't forget to make contact with personnel latterly as what you're doing may concern them and vice versa. Do the best you can as I have always thought if it's not worth doing right, it's not worth doing at all. Be aware of changing environments and the people you serve and keep being efficient and effective at doing the right thing right. I will close now, and I hope I have helped you in developing your own leadership and management style.